CONTENTS

ACKNOWLEDGEMENTS

This book could never have been written without the kindness of friends and family who helped to look after my three young children, and the understanding of those children when they heard, so often, 'Mummy's working'. These people include: Roger; Mom and Dad; Babs and Wyn; Alexis and Claudine; Violaine and Stephane; Celine and Jack; Nick and Caroline; Sonia; Florence; Nathalie and Michel; also Neil, who has helped me so much recently.

During the research for the book, the following teachers kindly gave me time to work alongside them and to discuss ideas together: Maggie Barrows (Christopher Rawlins CE Primary School, Adderbury); Di Cavill and Chris Roulstone (The Grange CP School, Banbury); Liz Cracknell and the nursery staff (St Barnabus CE First School, Oxford); Hilary Dilworth (Hardwick Primary School, Banbury); Ros Leather (Bishop Carpenter CE Primary School, North Newington); John Moffitt, Lynne Stephens and Margaret Sharpe (Deddington CE School); Nancy Padmore (Queen's Dyke Primary School, Witney); Rosie Roberts (Elms Road Nursery School, Botley). Also Trevor Easterbrook, Sally Abbey and Lynne Pointer of The Oxfordshire Mathematics Advisory Support Team (Oxfordshire Mathematics Centre, Woodeaton), Terri Jory (Cumnor C E Primary School) and Janet Duffin.

Suzanne Anderson typed the book so efficiently and Shirley Clarke has given me a great deal of support and encouragement throughout its creation.

DISCOVERING MATHEMATICS

with **4- to 7-year-olds**

Anna Lewis

Series Editor: Shirley Clarke

Hodder & Stoughton

A MEMBER OF THE HODDER HEADLINE GROUP

This book is dedicated to
Tristan, Oscar and Sébastien

British Library Cataloguing in Publication Data
A catalogue entry for this title is available from the British Library.

ISBN 0 340 60589 8

First published 1996
Impression number   10 9 8 7 6 5 4 3 2 1
Year   1999 1998 1997 1996

Typeset by Multiplex Techniques Ltd.
Printed in Great Britain for Hodder & Stoughton Educational, a division of Hodder Headline Plc, 338 Euston Road, London NW1 3BH by The Bath Press, Avon.

INTRODUCTION

This section includes:

CHAPTER 1 · LEARNING

WHAT IS LEARNING?

They do things differently in France. We moved to Normandy in 1991, and our children were immediately welcomed into the local village school – a 'classe unique', i.e. one dedicated, hard-working and marvellous teacher (who'd been there for twenty years) and nineteen pupils (aged between four and eleven) sitting in rows at worn-out, much carved, ancient, two-by-two desks. The atmosphere in many French schools seems peculiarly antiquated: children working in silence, no practical equipment, textbooks that their parents used, yellowing maps on the wall, unthinking copying from the blackboard (or each other), the adult knowing best, almost daily tests ('contrôles'), learning by rote, getting shaken or rapped across the knuckles if you forget or don't understand … There are many people in Britain who wish to revert to this educational style, but it crushes confidence, ignores initiative, cramps the imagination, destroys creativity, and, basically, it inspired me in writing this book, sharpening my ideas and beliefs.

Learning should never be:

- a chore;
- a worry (or fear);
- forced;
- something you do to please parents and teachers;
- something you do because you have to.

Instead it must be:

- engaging;
- interesting for its own sake;
- often self-driven;

- a welcome challenge;
- something that uses active, intelligent thinking.

Learning will not always be fun. But its difficulties should be embraced with self-confidence and energy, with an acceptance that, whilst effort, persistence and imagination can overcome most problems, there will still, on occasion, be dead ends or unsuccessful outcomes – and yet it doesn't matter!

'...the child who learns quickly is adventurous. She's ready to run risks ... She's not concerned with concealing her ignorance or protecting herself. She's ready to expose herself to disappointment and defeat. She has a certain confidence. She expects to make sense out of things sooner or later. She has a kind of trust.'

(John Holt, 1989)

Very young children are often like this, whether they are learning to walk or actively struggling to make sense of a new idea or word. Not only do they not mind about making so many errors along the way, but they are almost equally unmoved about the success when it comes. It's not the success, *per se*, that they enjoy – it's the new skill or understanding itself that is rewarding. Meanwhile, they will have already gone on to setting themselves the next challenge ... and the next.

'The personal qualities which pupils need to develop include:
- motivation and preparedness to tackle the unfamiliar and unknown – willingness to "have a go";
- flexibility and creative thinking in overcoming difficulties and developing new approaches;
- independence of thought and action ...'

(Non-Statutory Guidance B5.13, 1989)

Young children have lots of this already. When they come to school, we need to keep it, foster it, nurture it, and protect it.

Barbara Tizard and Martin Hughes (1984) compared the informal learning at home with the more formal learning of school. Their results emphasise the amazing intellectual learning of home, often not activity-based or play-based, but simply through talking in a leisurely way alongside everyday activities, real activities, such as eating lunch together or making a shopping list. At home, the children asked their parents an average of twenty-six questions an hour, compared to asking their teachers an average of two questions an hour. Of the school questions, the majority were 'business' questions, such as 'Where is the glue?' At home, they were mostly 'curiosity' and 'why?' questions, such as 'Why are the seats of chairs different shapes?'

'...much that children appeared to be learning from their mothers was not the consequence of deliberate teaching, ... the children themselves often played an active part in initiating learning by their questions.'

(Tizard and Hughes, 1984)

Intelligence and learning exist in young children well before they come to school. Even babies will persist at trying to grasp an object, unobserved, undaunted by so much failure, beyond praise or blame, just engrossed in their learning (whether anyone notices it or not). When I taught five-year-olds for the first time, I shall never forget being staggered by *every* child's intelligence and eagerness to learn, whatever their background, when they first came to school. Indeed, with no direct teaching, most children have already experienced and learned a substantial amount of mathematics before Year 1. For example: sorting (putting toys away, helping with laundry); measures (near/far, big/small, thick/thin, full/empty, hot/cold, fast/slow, deep, high, heavy, etc.); conservation (it's still the same amount of dinner although it's now cut up); number (verbal counting, number songs, seeing numbers around them, learning special numbers like house numbers or their age, using numbers in games, money, time, computers, etc.); shape and space (toy cars in straight paths, curved ones, under a table, around a corner, between chair legs, through a tunnel, roundness, flatness of blocks, fitting them together, up/down, backwards/forwards, round and round at the play park) etc. This experience and learning feeds directly into making sense of the mathematics they meet at school.

No matter how clear and patient your teacher, the process of learning can never be 'second hand', passed on to you from someone else. The learner has to be in control. When learning to use a new computer, it is not enough to watch someone else showing you what to do. You have to be doing it yourself, for real: exploring, making mistakes, trying something new, making your own discoveries about what it can do, needing to know something and being able to ask for what is needed.

A Year 1 teacher can define for the child what learning is all about in school and prevent them from losing their innate curiosity and desire to make sense of new experiences for themselves. The essence of this is allowing children:

- to offer and use their own ideas;
- to make choices;
- to ask questions that are followed up and taken seriously.

Teachers of older children often complain about the difficulty in getting their pupils to think for themselves and make their own decisions. They say things like 'if my children find it hard to use their own ideas and ask their own questions, then I'm sure younger children couldn't do it.' But it's the younger children who can do this best of all, and with the greatest confidence (from Year 1, school usually knocks it out of them and then tries to redevelop it later). For example, some Year 1 children planned to go outside to study the traffic and what kinds of vehicles went past their school. In pairs, a group of children were given large pieces of blank paper and some time to devise their own data-collection sheets beforehand. With no hesitation whatsoever, they enthusiastically discussed ideas and set about the task. Everyone's sheets were different and extremely interesting to look at and discuss together afterwards (figure 1.1).

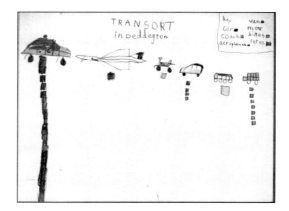

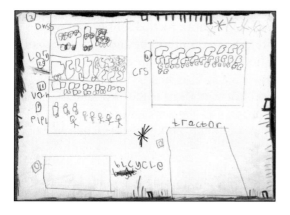

FIGURE 1.1 *Variety of data-collection sheets, Year 1*

- 'You were all together; have you all got the same results? Why? Why not? Does it matter?'
- 'Which sheet shows the numbers of each type of vehicle best? For comparison?'
- 'Did you all look for the same vehicles?'
- 'What classifications were used?'
- 'What were there none of?'
- 'Which was the easiest/hardest to complete? Why?'

The sheer variety of response gave rise to a whole range of mathematical learning. If the teacher had devised the sheets (or simply 'helped' or 'interfered' more in their construction), we might never have seen categories for fighter jets, people, bikes, tractors, ambulances, etc., and the variety of vertical, horizontal, boxed, pictorial, symbolic representation and use of keys in their designs. Interesting too, that the information is sometimes recorded from right to left or top to bottom – perfectly valid ways to form their charts and so rarely seen in any published mathematics materials. There was no concern or worry in evidence on the part of these children that they might be doing it the wrong way or that they should all be doing it the same way. They enjoyed seeing different approaches to the same problem afterwards and made no judgements about whose was best (except in the discussion of 'best' for particular purposes).

From Year 1, if children meet mathematical tasks that are open enough for them to bring their imaginations to bear, to make use of their ideas and their experience, then the resulting variety of response will foster creativity by sharing different ways of thinking, and will encourage children's own questions and intrigue. (I have only ever taught one five-year-old who didn't have this confidence to offer ideas and make her own decisions, once settled into the class. She had transferred from a more formal school and was already entrenched in the expectation of right and wrong answers, right and wrong ways of doing things. She was intelligent, successful and already scared of failure, being therefore totally dependent upon me or other children in all her work. The damage can be undone, but it is a long process to rebuild confidence in being an independent thinker and learner.)

'How often do we allow four- and five-year-olds the freedom to take initiatives within activities which we set up under the label of "mathematics"?'

(Marion Bird, 1991)

When they are free to explore within an activity, children are usually extremely good at setting themselves just the right challenges. If they retain confidence in themselves as explorers or learners, then they will enjoy trying things out in mathematics and will actively search for interesting patterns and relationships (see page 11). The mathematics they meet needs to be a collection of starting points that engages their interest and, taken together, covers the Programmes of Study.

When children make sense of their environment for themselves – exploring, trying things out, asking questions, relating it to previous experiences and understandings – then they do not forget what they absorb and learn. It's assimilated into their own mental model and will be used to relate to other explorations later on. Children love learning and are extremely good at it when they are in control of it like this. They will not mind 'getting stuck' or meeting inconsistencies, because they are confident enough to try different strategies, ask the right questions, correct themselves if necessary and challenge themselves to sort it all out. They can justify and explain their work because it arises from their own thinking, their own inquisitiveness.

Real learning is a pleasure in itself. Children don't need praise for it. We need to let it happen almost unnoticed, simply sharing the child's fascination when they invite us to do so. You can't make children learn. The child has to do it.

BASIC PRINCIPLES OF LEARNING

Children of all ages and abilities need, in their learning, to:

- be in control;
- make some choices/decisions;
- use their own ideas and imaginations;
- have a purpose or reason to learn that engages their interest;
- explore and play with ideas;
- know that school expects them to think for themselves;
- have confidence and self-respect;
- enjoy the challenge of confusion and things going wrong;
- challenge themselves;
- be able to justify and explain;
- record their work in their own way;
- check and be sure;
- share and learn from each other.

Throughout this book, the ideas for learning about mathematics are offered for you and your children to enjoy, explore, adapt and talk about. There should be a rather informal delight in discovering the regularities and patterns of mathematics alongside intrigue and surprise when things don't seem to fit the rule. The curiosity of the young child at home needs to come into school and apply itself to the wonders of mathematics.

'…when we use a child's natural desire to explore the new and unknown, and to gain some control over it, without trying to force him faster or further than he feels ready to go, both pupil and teacher have the most fun and make the most progress.'

(John Holt, 1967)

CHAPTER 2

UNDERSTANDING MATHEMATICS

This chapter includes:
- Introduction
- What is mathematics?
- Using and Applying mathematics
- Progression
- The CAN Curriculum
- Conclusion

'… at school we are often led … to a style of teaching which is content-driven, and to the use of documentation as a syllabus on which we think we can rely to reassure us as to an expected order, progression and development. An alternative approach is to focus on the journey, rather than the destination. This shifts the emphasis from the syllabus, and consequently the teacher, to the learner and leaves us expecting differences in inputs, aptitudes, interests, expectations and consequently in outcomes. It causes us to rethink the mathematics curriculum as an exploration of the mathematical world.'

(Leone Burton, 1994)

INTRODUCTION

This chapter revolves around the Programme of Study for Using and Applying Mathematics (hereafter referred to as 'Using and Applying'). The cornerstone of the whole Key Stage 1 Mathematics curriculum is giving pupils opportunities to:

- use and apply mathematics in practical tasks, real-life problems and within mathematics itself;
- explain their thinking to support the development of their reasoning.

This captures the essence of what it means to be a mathematician, for all ages and abilities. It is easy to see that the Cockcroft Report's (1982) recommendations for children experiencing mathematics through practical work, problem solving, investigational work and discussion are embodied here. The recommendation that there should be some exposition is less important at Key Stage 1 than perhaps in later key stages, and the recommendation for practice and consolidation is subsumed within these approaches because ideas will be practised and consolidated by *using and applying* them in a whole variety of contexts. This is how it should be.

Research into learning mathematics shows that children do not learn in a neat, linear, step-by-step fashion; instead, they make unexpected leaps and connections within a network of concepts (e.g. Brenda Denvir and Margaret Brown 1986).

Fortunately, the initial fragmented, level-by-level structure of the National Curriculum has been replaced by Programmes of Study which span the whole key stage. Using and Applying now brings experience and research together for the first time and allows the child to be the focus of the mathematics curriculum. Using and Applying is the key to the development of mathematical thinking. It *is* mathematics.

WHAT IS MATHEMATICS?

As most of us received such a distorted view of the subject in our own schooling, it is difficult to understand the concept of mathematics with any confidence. Teaching mathematics can be rather like having to teach visitors to a wildlife park all about snakes when we have a phobia about them ourselves. Of course, the terror is caused by misapprehensions and misunderstandings. (Snakes are mistakenly thought to be horribly slimy by anyone without any real experience of them.) Even if you are not frightened by mathematics, even if you enjoy it, it can still be difficult to define and describe what the subject is all about.

Like all good learning, the best way to develop a better understanding of mathematics is to experience it for yourself in a variety of ways, and then to think about or analyse what you've been doing. Mathematics is often described as:

- patterns and relationships;
- intelligent thinking and reasoning;
- a network of interrelated concepts.

But these words will mean nothing unless you can relate your own experiences to them; and yet, if I were to describe mathematics in terms of a set of rules and procedures to be remembered and practised for examinations, together with some abstract, algebraic symbolisation, many people would recognise this as the mathematics they have experienced at school.

Patterns and investigating

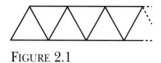

FIGURE 2.1

To experience some real mathematics and to reflect on the mathematical thinking involved, try this activity on your own and/or with some children.

- Draw a very long line of interlocking triangles (figure 2.1).
- Choose a sequence of numbers to write inside them (figure 2.2).

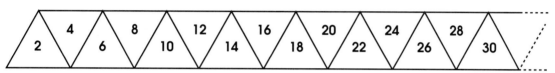

FIGURE 2.2 *'Snake' of triangles*

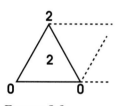

FIGURE 2.3

- Now choose three numbers to put around the first triangle so that they total the number inside it (figure 2.3).
- Continue along the line and look for patterns.
- Try predicting the next few numbers, and checking to see if the pattern holds – what if you changed the order of your starter numbers?; What if you used negative numbers?; What about a different sequence?

In terms of Using and Applying, this activity focuses on investigating within mathematics itself. It is likely that you were:

- selecting and using the appropriate mathematics (e.g. using multiplication tables or number sequences or odd/even number patterns, mentally adding two numbers and finding the difference between that and the total for the triangle by adding on or subtracting ...);
- recognising simple patterns and relationships and making related predictions about them (e.g. noticing a spatial relationship within a number pattern that is produced);
- asking questions, including 'What would happen if ...?' and 'Why?' (e.g. What if I put the same number in each triangle? What if I used fractions?).

If you ask a colleague or family friend to try this activity, you may see how the same starting point can lead to different aspects of mathematics. By sharing your ideas with each other, you may think of something else to explore and be intrigued by. Why does it work? Are there always patterns, whatever you do?

If you became involved in this 'snake' of triangles activity, you will be able to see how mathematics can be a creation of (or search for) patterns and relationships.

Intelligence and problem-solving

If you prefer solving practical problems to investigating in such an open-ended way, you could think about solving a real-life problem, e.g. parcelling up a gift to send in the post. In terms of Using and Applying you are likely to:

- select appropriate materials (e.g. Which shape and size of box or jiffy bag would be best from what I have available? How much string will I need to cut?);
- use different mathematical approaches in looking for ways to overcome difficulties (e.g. Would the brown paper cover the box better if I turned it diagonally? If I fill the spaces in the box with one, two, three sheets of crumpled newspaper, would it stop the gift rattling around?).

In this type of real-life activity (likewise for things like planning a journey, mending the car, wallpapering, sorting out family finances, etc.), you will be able to see how mathematics can be a mental tool for intelligent thinking and reasoning.

Network of concepts

In both examples above, it is likely that connections will be made between different areas of mathematics, helping to form a network, or structure, of interrelated concepts. For example, in the 'snake' of triangles activity, the following aspects of mathematics content could be related (figure 2.4.)

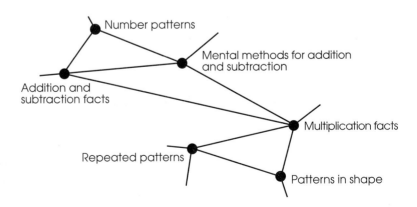

FIGURE 2.4 *Related aspects of mathematics in 'snake' of triangles activity*

In parcelling up a gift to post, there could also be links between many different aspects of mathematics (figure 2.5).

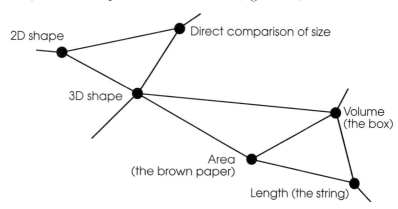

FIGURE 2.5

It is possible to make amazingly complicated networks out of all the possible relationships between each concept in mathematics, spiralling upwards through different levels of development like a molecule of DNA. A teacher does not need to be an expert in the structure of mathematics concepts, how each develops and relates to every other structure, in order to teach excellent mathematics. (Like a GP, who can diagnose and treat his patients but does not need to know the molecular structure of DNA when interacting with people and their illnesses.) It is sufficient to know that it is there, and that the children, in learning about mathematics, will (with the help of Using and Applying) be creating these connections for themselves, within their own developing network of mathematical understanding. Using and Applying is the means for this to occur. Without it, children will develop a knowledge of some of the concepts and some of the connections in an isolated way and will not grow intellectually as mathematicians. (Richard Skemp has invented a marvellous analogy of 'real' mathematics being like exploring a town, constructing a mental map of the buildings and routes between them, rather than following and trying to remember a set of specific directions between certain predetermined sites.)

USING AND APPLYING MATHEMATICS

Given that I believe Using and Applying represents the basis of mathematical thinking, its very title could be interpreted as using and applying this thinking *to* the content areas of Number and Shape, Space and Measures. Indeed, Using and Applying works alongside the other Programmes of Study all the time. It is not distinct and separate – something to do *after* number, shape, space or measures work has been learned.

'Though applications are derived from more fundamental ideas, *this does not determine their order of presentation to young children*. We can begin with an idea and then apply it, or introduce children to applications and thereby give them experience of a fundamental idea in action.'

(Clemson and Clemson, 1994)

Young children need to experience fundamental ideas in action, not in isolation. We always make the mistake of unravelling mathematics to find the fundamental idea that can be the simplified starting point. But the unravelling itself is the best part of the mathematics! When we sort out the mathematical ideas on their behalf and present them in isolation (in order to apply them later), we are denying children this active, intelligent learning. It's like going on a treasure hunt and some terribly kind person finding and giving the treasure to you, not understanding that there's more fun in the quest than the resulting prize. Using and Applying Mathematics is a means of creating and 'managing' activities that are much more like treasure hunts.

Using and Applying is not something that we can assume is happening all the time in Key Stage 1 classes (because of the amount of practical materials and discussion often found there) and ignore it except for assessment purposes. It should be the driving force of our teaching. It is a summary of all the different definitions of mathematics. It brings together, coherently, ideas of pattern and relationships, logical reasoning, language and symbolisation, problem-solving strategies, investigation and practical mathematics. It has pure mathematics and applied mathematics within it. It combines mathematical thinking and ways of working with the variety of contexts that are necessary for these to develop. The active process of teaching and learning mathematics in the classroom is captured in Using and Applying. Outside the classroom, we can focus more upon Number and Shape, Space and Measures in our planning and evaluating. (Not exclusively so, but in terms of main emphasis (figure 2.6).)

It is because Using and Applying does so many things for mathematics teaching that a) it will not go away; and b) it seems so difficult to understand and use. It enables the structuring to occur that makes sense of mathematics for each person. It is so important that it is even built into the Programmes of Study for ATs 2 and 3 as well as existing on its own. Most of the statements include phrases such as:

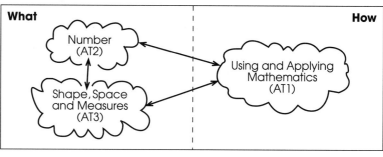

FIGURE 2.6
Mathematical focus in planning and interacting with children

develop flexible methods;
use a variety of practical resources and contexts;
explore … realistic data;
record in a variety of ways … relate to;
use, explore, record patterns … and sequences;
use in context … purposeful contexts;
develop a range of mental methods;
make predictions;
solve problems;
choose a suitable method … choose units;
check answers in different ways;
describe and discuss;
compare objects and events;
interpret.

- develop flexible methods;
- use a variety of practical resources and contexts;
- explore … realistic data;
- record in a variety of ways … relate to;
- use, explore, record patterns … and sequences;
- use in context … purposeful contexts;
- develop a range of mental methods;
- make predictions;
- solve problems;
- choose a suitable method … choose units;
- check answers in different ways;
- describe and discuss;
- compare objects and events;
- interpret.

The Programmes of Study for ATs 2 and 3 are already saturated with Using and Applying. Children cannot do these things unless they are 'in control' of their work, deciding and reasoning for themselves.

'The National Curriculum requires all schools to […] develop a teaching and learning approach in which the uses and applications of mathematics permeate and influence all work in mathematics. This is a major undertaking for schools, and perhaps the single most significant challenge for the teaching of mathematics required by the National Curriculum in its aim for raising standards for all pupils'.

(Non-Statutory Guidance D5, 1989)

Mathematical thinking

Mathematics used to be taught in a step-by-step way, where each aspect was studied separately as a 'practice' of facts, rules and procedures. Early-years teachers have often brought different aspects of mathematics together by studying Pattern, Sorting and Classifying, and Comparing as higher-order themes to apply to number, shape and measurement. (The Key Stage 1 Programme of Study also emphasises the overall importance of these themes in its first paragraph.)

Using and Applying shifts the focus of mathematics further onto the development of mathematical thinking in the child. By thinking mathematically, children can search for patterns, sort, classify and compare for themselves. (We need to step back a little more and offer activities that facilitate and enable children to be in control of doing this.) The three strands of Using and Applying are:

- making and monitoring decisions to solve problems;
- developing mathematical language and communication;
- developing mathematical reasoning.

These are inextricably linked and together make up the 'real power' of mathematics (Using and Applying, NCC Book A). They represent a way of teaching that allows children to think mathematically and 'be mathematicians', whatever their age or ability.

Can reception children do it?

If mathematics is a slightly higher level of mental activity than has previously been thought, you may wonder how reception, Year 1 and Year 2 children can do it at all. But they are doing it already and have been doing so for years; it just hasn't normally been called mathematics before.

As described in chapter 1, young children are naturally curious and desperate to learn. The Key Stage 1 Programme of Study for AT1 could be seen as trying to capture some of the ways young children learn, and harness them to mathematics.

When children are freely playing, they are using a whole array of mathematical thinking skills. For example, in building with bricks, they will quite naturally be:

- *deciding* which bricks to use (depending on the shape and size required);
- *imagining* what the shape/structure represents and thinking ahead;
- *reasoning*: 'If you put that on now, it'll fall over. Wait till I've done this side';
- *predicting*: 'I think it'll be bigger than me';
- *planning*: 'Let's do a side each. Then we can put the bridge across';

FIGURE 2.7

- *trying other ways/getting unstuck*: 'Oh, it just won't balance ...
  Let's try that flatter one';
- *recording*: 'I'm going to draw a picture of our ... It's really
  good. Then we can do it again'.

When any of us, children included, are exploring new materials,
solving practical problems, making something, playing with games
and puzzles, engaged in any activity (physical or mental) that uses
mathematics in our daily lives, we will be 'practising' our
mathematical thinking. In the building bricks example (and the
parcelling up of a gift example), connections between ideas of
shape and measurement are being actively explored. We are, all of
us, at all ages, already highly skilled mathematicians. We just
haven't often learned it in our mathematics lessons!

We must not 'simplify' the mathematics we offer to Key Stage 1
children by taking the thinking out of the tasks. Young children
can be highly adept at mathematical thinking (whilst their
experiences of the content move ahead on a broad front). In an
activity to find and record how many different ways five multilink
could be fixed together, it was the younger children in the group
who had better ideas for organising the task. They said things like,
'We won't do twists because there would be so many' or 'We'll
only do shapes that can lie flat on the table'. They were setting the
parameters for the investigation and also justifying every model as
they went. This is not at all unusual.

FIGURE 2.8

The words of mathematics

Mathematics is sometimes described as a language for
communicating abstract ideas and for operating on abstract
relationships. It is made up of special words, diagrams and
symbols that represent concepts. Words are the first symbols that
are used to represent a mathematical idea. But beware! Just
because a child is using a mathematical word, it does not mean

FIGURE 2.9 *Triangle* *'mistakes'*

that he or she understands it. For example, children often use the word 'triangle' correctly to describe an equilateral triangle. But when I tried asking a group of five- and six-year-olds if the shapes in figure 2.9 were triangles, they laughed at all my 'mistakes'! From their practical experience with logiblocs, they seriously didn't think that anything other than an equilateral triangle, the right way up, could be properly called a triangle. It is for this reason that we should always question and challenge even the simplest ideas with young children, even when we know they are correct, and also be sure to place every mathematical concept into a wide variety of contexts. (It was not enough to learn the names of shapes from using logiblocs.)

Sometimes several words or symbols can have the same meaning too (e.g. subtract, – , count back, take away, minus, fewer, etc.). Schools should *never* decide to use a particular word in preference to others throughout Years 1 to 3 (and beyond) in order to avoid confusion. Children need to learn that all these words are different ways of saying the same thing. Confusion should be embraced and explored in mathematics at every level. A variety of mathematics schemes and resources will have mathematical language used in different ways. Each class *needs* this variety.

Children's own recording

If mathematical language (words, symbols, diagrams) labels concepts and represents our thinking, it must be right that children should record their thinking in their own way (to try to match and communicate what they actually did in their minds) before they use more formal methods. Using standard forms of recording too early can disguise misunderstandings. It is possible to learn to read and write words (as a decoding skill) without understanding their meaning. Similarly, it is possible to learn to read and write mathematical words and symbols (as procedural skills) without understanding. To put more emphasis on meaning in reading and writing, we have learned to accept child-devised, 'invented', non-standard words that gradually develop into the standard, 'correct' ways to read and write (e.g. Emergent Writing). We also need to learn to accept and encourage 'Emergent Mathematics'. Children who invent their own ways to convey mathematical meaning will understand mathematics far better than those who don't. It is a tiny thing to attach the conventional label to something that is already understood. It is far harder to use the conventional label to teach for understanding. For example, after collecting together all the words and symbols that the children have devised to represent the active process of addition, it is easy to contribute the conventional sign + (e.g. 3 + 4) to the collection, if it hasn't already been offered by a child who is familiar with a calculator. In contrast, a child was having great difficulty with his sums in one class because he wasn't quite sure what '+' meant. He'd been told that he had to get three cubes and then four cubes and then see how many he had. His results were consistently his second number of cubes, as that's what he always had in his hand at the end:

$$3 + 4 = 4$$
$$2 + 5 = 5$$
$$4 + 3 = 3$$
$$5 + 5 = 5$$

Even the children who were adding correctly often did not know what the symbols meant.

Remembering facts

Facts in mathematics range from the conventional way to write the numerals to the results of certain operations on numbers. All are important to remember, but none of them needs to be learned by rote, or practised out of context. Skemp estimates that about ninety-five per cent of mathematics uses intelligent learning and only about five per cent uses 'habit learning'. The facts to remember in mathematics can be learned by using them in so many ways that they become second nature, using them 'habitually'.

Very few of the facts that make up five per cent of mathematics ever need to be told to children. Most of them can and should be explored and discovered, used and applied. This doesn't mean that you can never tell a child anything in mathematics. If a fact is the purpose or focus of an activity, then we should help children to find their own ways to explore it. (Telling them might spoil the whole activity.) But if a fact is needed that is secondary to the purpose of the activity, it *can* be given and *should* be given, especially if the flow of the mathematical thinking is likely to be interrupted (e.g. Oscar, age five, was concentrating on a simple calculator game and needed to know if 5 was a two or a five. It would not have been appropriate to have sent him around the classroom looking at numerals to try to find out for himself. He needed to know quickly so that he could continue the game, from which he was learning about the sequence of numbers). If the focus is on the numerals themselves, then they should be explored and discovered for their great variety, not told or practised endlessly in the same style in worksheets. Numerals can look very different on clocks, calculators, books, notes, number lines, etc. What is it that's the same about all these threes? What's different? What matters and doesn't matter about writing a numeral three (figure 2.10)?

FIGURE 2.10 *The numeral three*

Facts are often arbitrary and sometimes strange. The way we say the teen numbers doesn't match the way in which they are written. Eighteen, for example, sounds as if the eight should be written first. (French children say 'dix-huit', (ten, eight) for eighteen, but have to cope with 'soixante-dix' or 'sixty-ten' instead of 'seventy', which isn't arbitrary, but does seem a little odd to us, when seventy is simpler.)

Number facts can all be discovered (or worked out) and used in the context of games, investigations, shopping, etc. It is more efficient to learn them this way, because no special time is needed; they are learned as a 'side-effect' of learning about number patterns, relationships, calculating methods, and so on.

Not only facts, but any mathematics can be consolidated by being used and applied in a variety of contexts. Practise and memory in mathematics are embraced by Using and Applying and subsumed into higher levels of mathematical thinking.

'"Open" activities require pupils to employ a wide range of strategies [...] whilst retaining the elements of consolidation and practise of knowledge and skills.'

(Non-Statutory Guidance 3.3 D6, 1989)

PROGRESSION

Regions of experience

Because mathematics is a network of interconnected ideas, and because children need to make their own connections through Using and Applying (making some decisions for themselves and exploring within more 'open' tasks), it is totally inappropriate to offer mathematics to children in a step-by-step, linear fashion. Just as it is possible to draw a complex network of interrelated mathematics which we cannot teach from, it is possible to teach from a hierarchical list of mathematics which children cannot learn from. Not only do they need to have activities which provide the opportunity to bring together different aspects of mathematics, but they also need to be able to work at different levels within an activity, challenging themselves and/or consolidating something.

'For all the time we ourselves impose limits on tasks, we are in danger of not doing justice to children's potential.'

(M. Bird, 1991)

This is why the Programme of Study has been organised in Key Stages instead of levels. For teaching and learning in the classroom, we need to offer banks of activities that can span several levels within the Key Stage. This all leads to a 'non-linear' mathematics curriculum. It provides the basis for a set of regions or networks of experience to explore within. The level-by-level development of mathematics (and the hierarchy within and between levels that it is possible to identify) is a structure to map assessment on to, but not to teach from.

'I assumed that the sequence used in children's textbooks represented the most successful model. Years of research with children have convinced me that this model is a successful and necessary tool for writing a textbook, but not for learning [...] Experience with children in *their* world does not show this sequence at all [...] Our children's world is not linear (one idea isolated and presented repeatedly until mastery); rather, it is geometric (many, many ideas presented simultaneously, half understood by the child, with each idea contributing to the growth of the other ideas, until the "light dawns" and makes clear several ideas at once).'

(Mary Baratta-Lorton, 1976)

When young children are learning to talk, it is possible to identify a linear hierarchy that describes for us the progression in their development. For example, they will make one-syllable utterances before putting two syllables together; they will name things before they can begin to construct basic sentences; their sentences will become more sophisticated, etc. But we don't follow such a step-by-step progression as parents in helping them to learn to talk. We don't decide whether our child is 'ready' to experience two-syllable words before we speak to them in words of more than one syllable. We don't wait until they've remembered a certain number of names for things and used them in lots of contexts before we begin work on verbs or sentences. Instead, we provide a world of talk, with all its meanings and purposes, within which our children can actively take part, intellectually, in making sense of it all for themselves. (Interestingly, they use many mathematical thinking skills in the process: trial and error; conjecturing; testing; checking; looking for patterns, rules and relationships; etc.) We do facilitate this process by relating words directly to the child's own experiences (e.g. 'Mummy put your shoes on') and adapting our language appropriately. But the focus of talk is almost always to convey meaning, and factual inaccuracies or 'incorrect' speech will usually only be corrected (quietly and in context, by repeating the utterance with its intended meaning) if it matters, not practised endlessly (out of context) before going on to the next stage. And so it should be with mathematics.

For English
'If you concentrate on communicating, everything else will follow.'
(Roger Brown)

For Mathematics
'If you concentrate on Using and Applying, everything else will follow.'
(Anna Lewis)

When children are measuring for a purpose, for example, they may choose to use direct comparison if it is the most appropriate way. Adults frequently use direct comparison in daily life (e.g. finding an envelope of the right size). If non-standard or standard units are required, then it will be for a reason. Children should build a *cumulative* range of measuring skills that they can choose from and understand how they each relate, not move down the line practising more complex skills and never looking back. Using and Applying enables the learner to go backwards and forwards through the traditional hierarchy as appropriate. Children need to work within a region of experience (e.g. measuring for a purpose, number patterns, properties of shapes) that allows for different levels and different aspects of related mathematics. The structure of your planning is then based around a mathematics theme, or sets of objectives that work well together, creating banks of activities which can often be done in any order.

Rates of progress

'Mathematics takes a long time to learn because of the necessity of building up relationships between different ideas and between different aspects of the same idea.'
(SCAA)

It is vital that we don't rush ahead too quickly in mathematics at Key Stage 1. Children need time to build a very wide and strong foundation for their 'tower of understanding' in mathematics.

Challenges for more able children can and should often be offered 'sideways', helping them to make an even more secure base from which to build an even taller tower in the future (figure 2.11).

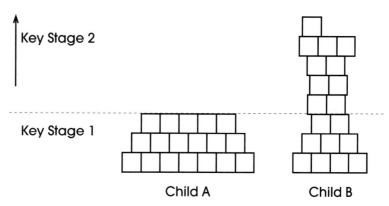

FIGURE 2.11 *Towers of understanding in mathematics*

By offering mathematics that is open-ended enough to allow responses at different levels and by having high expectations of the children, child A will push ahead into new realms of mathematics whilst at the same time consolidating and relating new ideas to the base. Child B has been pushed ahead by his teacher and appears to cope quite well superficially, but is not in confident control of his learning, and will sooner or later lose confidence completely in mathematics as the tower becomes more insecure and shaky.

The Programme of Study for Key Stage 1 includes aspects of mathematics that lead to achievement at level 3. There will be many children who are ready to meet this mathematics towards the end of the Key Stage, and can begin to explore these new ideas. But for most children, it is only a beginning. I have met very few Key Stage 1 children who could be assessed as having achieved level 3 in any mathematics Attainment Target, at least not confidently and properly, having spent a reasonable amount of time exploring the mathematics, relating it to other aspects of mathematics, using it all in a variety of contexts, and consolidating it whilst working towards an understanding of some of the mathematics which leads to level 4. (There is a danger that, because the Programme of Study at Key Stage 1 includes level 3, teachers and parents might expect mastery.)

Differentiation

We need Using and Applying to help us with progression and differentiation. However good our assessment techniques, we will never be able to see the internal structure of mathematical understanding that each child possesses; and even if we could, we'd never know what connections are about to be made next, however precise our activities. How can we know when each child is ready? For example, young children are often asked to 'count on from the larger number' far too soon in simple additions. Pamela Liebeck offers a good way to put yourself in your children's place for a while. You know the sequence of letters in the alphabet probably as well as most young children know the sequence of numbers, so imagine that the numbers are changed so that a, b, c, d, ... represent 1, 2, 3, 4 ... Now, without translating back to numbers, try to work out 'c more than e'. It is very difficult to start at e and count on a, b, c, and most people find themselves counting a, b, c, d, e, ... f, g, h (i.e. going back to the beginning of the counting sequence, 'just to make sure'). The real problem here is in the nature of the task. Counting on from the larger number is a strategy for more efficient calculating, and we can never know exactly when a child is ready for it. (We mustn't force them into it.) The task, incorporating Using and Applying, would be more like: 'How many different ways can we find to work out and show 5 + 3?' A table-top display could be created to show all the children's ideas. You could add some ideas yourself. Counting on from five will be represented somewhere (figure 2.12) and talked about. Those children who can, will assimilate the idea into their thinking.

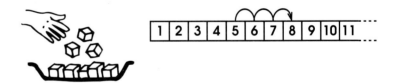

FIGURE 2.12 *Show a sum*

Through more open activities (where they make their own decisions about what they do), children can explore new ideas at exactly the right level for them. One set of activities (or one activity) can serve children who are at very different stages in their learning. And an extra benefit is that they can talk to each other and learn from each other because they've been working from the same starting point.

THE CAN CURRICULUM

> 'Project teachers have acquired an enormous respect for the children's ingenuity, persistence and enjoyment of number, once the shackles of a traditional scheme of work have been taken away.'
>
> (Hilary Shuard, 1991)

Open-endedness

An extremely well-tried and tested Using and Applying mathematics curriculum that excludes all forms of standard 'sums' and algorithms (e.g. tens and units sums arranged vertically) is the CAN (Calculator-Aware Number) Curriculum, which was developed in 1986 by Hilary Shuard *et al.* as part of the PrIME Project; it ran officially for six years and continues in many schools today. It is calculator-aware, *not* calculator led. Children have access to calculators at all times (from reception onwards) and are never told or taught how to do a calculation (or 'sum') with any particular formal pencil-and-paper method. Instead, they explore and investigate numbers, with a whole range of teacher and child-devised starting points, inventing their own calculating methods. There is a huge emphasis on mental arithmetic, and although the calculator is there, the children *don't* choose to use it when they can work something out quicker in their heads. The emphasis of the CAN Curriculum is not really on the calculator. Its biggest emphasis is on the open-ended exploration of number, in which the calculator is a very useful tool.

The basics

The 'basics' of calculating in the CAN Project are dealt with entirely through exploration, or Using and Applying. Children are encouraged to share all their different ways of working with numbers, and the vast majority of methods operate from left to right (e.g. 36 and 12 would be calculated as 30 and 10, before adding the 6 and 2). There are no pages of 'sums' for consolidation because children learn and practise their calculating by using and applying it from the beginning.

One of the first and most famous activities to emerge was 'shape sums', where children draw a square, for example, choose a number to put inside it and then try to find four numbers to put on the corners that will total to the number inside (figure 2.13).

With this starting point, a whole series of things can happen:

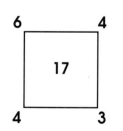

FIGURE 2.13 *Shape sums*

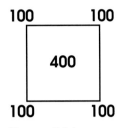

FIGURE 2.14

- Very young children often start choosing to use much larger numbers (figure 2.14).
- There are often surprises for the teacher, e.g. Gary's teacher 'had not yet "done" any work with these six-year-old children on place value in hundreds. However, Gary seemed to have found out how to decompose a three-digit number into hundreds, tens and units, although he was not yet sure which way round to write 7' (figure 2.15).

(From *Calculators, Children and Mathematics*, PrIME, 1991)

- Children begin to explore number patterns and relationships (figure 2.16).

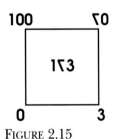

FIGURE 2.15

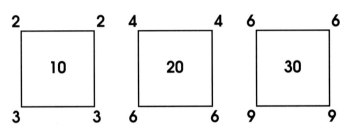

FIGURE 2.16

- Ideas of multiplication and division emerge (figure 2.17).

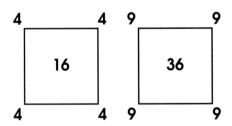

FIGURE 2.17

- The idea can work with negative numbers or subtraction (figure 2.18).

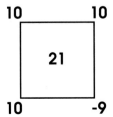

FIGURE 2.18

- Or fractions and decimals (figure 2.19).

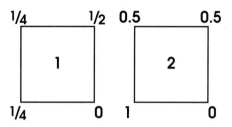

F<small>IGURE</small> 2.19

- Sometimes major discoveries are made. After writing 600, 700, 800 and 900, Molly (age six) said '... ten hundred ... but that looks like a thousand?! It *is* a thousand. So ten hundred is really one thousand! Wow!' (figure 2.20).

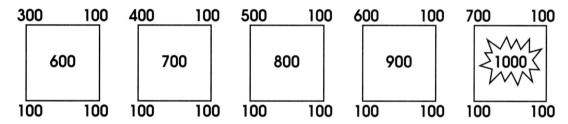

F<small>IGURE</small> 2.20

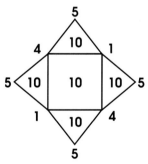

F<small>IGURE</small> 2.21

The calculator doesn't always feature very much in this activity, though some children do use it to check and explore. The main focus is a mental/abstract exploration with numbers and how they behave. (There isn't usually any practical equipment, though some children occasionally use it to build towers for each number on each corner.) The activity can be extended easily to different, straight-sided shapes, providing more or fewer corner numbers. The shapes can be fitted together to create puzzles where corners are shared (figure 2.21).

By choosing to use the same number inside all the shapes, a focus upon number bonds is created (an example of a constraint which can lead to a greater depth of investigation).

This whole activity demonstrates how young children can become engrossed in pure mathematics, for its own sake. They are *playing* within a mathematical context. A Using and Applying mathematics curriculum at Key Stage 1 will have many such open-ended 'starters'. Its success lies in the children being in control of what aspects of content they explore. It is not the context of the squares that is so interesting to the children, it is the amount of choice and freedom to explore.

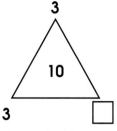

FIGURE 2.22

(Note: One teacher tried this activity as a closed worksheet to practise number bonds to 10. Each shape only had one number to find (figure 2.22). The children finished the activity dutifully but nothing else came from it.)

Teaching style

A Using and Applying curriculum needs to operate alongside a teaching style that uses open-ended questioning which will encourage and support children making decisions and thinking things out for themselves (see chapter 9). Many teachers who have been following a CAN Curriculum have noticed a huge shift or development in their roles and styles of teaching.

'Teaching style became less prescriptive, more facilitating, more one designed to observe and bring out the children's own mathematical skills and strategies than to impose the teacher's on them.'

(*Calculators in the Classroom*, Janet Duffin, 1993)

The CAN Curriculum provides a real picture of a Using and Applying mathematics curriculum in action. It tackles the 'basics' in mathematics (e.g. sums, number facts, multiplication tables, etc.) in a totally new and entirely appropriate way. It is more 'progressive' than any previous method and yet is at the heart of mathematics – and encouraged by government legislation! If number work can be done so well through Using and Applying, then all mathematics can.

CONCLUSION

What is so good about a Using and Applying mathematics curriculum?

FOR THE CHILDREN

- Mathematics is more closely related to children's own thinking and experiences.
- Mathematics becomes something that *all* children can do.
- Children are recognised for already being mathematicians, able to think mathematically for themselves.
- Children can make links between different aspects of mathematics.
- Mathematics is related to other areas of the curriculum.
- Children can learn from and help each other more.
- Mathematics can be imagined and talked about.

- Mathematics stops being 'sums' and which workbook, workcard or text you are on.
- Children become actively involved, in control of the mathematics they are doing (instead of having mathematics done to them).
- Children become more independent, less reliant on the teacher.
- Children are motivated by the mathematics (no external rewards necessary).
- Mathematics stops being about right and wrong answers.
- Children evaluate, reflect and think more about what they do.
- Children take initiatives and try out their own ideas.

'… work which is triggered by pupils themselves leads to better motivation and understanding.'

(Non-Statutory Guidance, 1989)

FOR THE TEACHER

- There are fewer 'queues' of children needing help.
- There is more opportunity to observe and assess.
- Mathematics is matched much more easily to children's own levels of ability (differentiation by outcome).
- There are fewer behavioural/discipline problems.
- There are opportunities to learn about real mathematics yourself and become excited by it.
- You don't have to know all the answers – the children explain and correct themselves.
- You don't have to prepare all the materials all the time (the children will mostly do it).
- You don't need to stick to one set of materials (e.g. one published scheme); variety is good.
- Mathematics becomes more manageable (because the children are not so dependent upon you).
- There are economies in learning/teaching time, as several things are experienced within each activity.

THE TEN BASIC PRINCIPLES OF A USING AND APPLYING MATHEMATICS CURRICULUM

1 The teacher uses open-ended questioning, enabling the children to use their own ideas and make their own decisions.

2 The majority of activities offered will be 'open' (in varying degrees).

3 Mathematics will be related to children's own experiences (whether real or imagined).

4   Children will use a variety of contexts (e.g. mathematical equipment, everyday objects, mental imagery, the indoor and outdoor environment, the children themselves, calculators, computers, programmable toys, etc.).

5   Children will record their work in their own way.

6   There will be much mathematical talk and discussion (between the children themselves and between teacher and pupils).

7   Mistakes, problems, dead-ends, confusion … will all be welcomed as discussion points, provoking reflection, self-evaluation, intrigue, checking or further ideas.

8   Problem-solving and investigational activities will be discussed for the mathematical thinking and ways of working that were involved, rather than any specific end result.

9   Most mathematics will be done for a purpose or reason (even if that reason is simply interest) that the children can specify. There are no artificial contexts.

10 The children will be motivated by the task and the mathematics itself. No external rewards will be necessary (e.g. stars, ticks, pleasing parents or teachers).

SECTION

A

THE HIDDEN MATHEMATICS CURRICULUM

This section includes:

Introduction

INTRODUCTION TO SECTION A

Mathematics is hiding all around you in your classroom, waiting to be discovered. You are probably aware of many hiding places, but have been too busy with the demands of the National Curriculum to seek them out. In this part of the book, I'd like to take you around your own class looking at some of this hidden mathematics and giving it full National Curriculum status.

A teacher recently told me the following story.

'I had only ever mentioned odds and evens informally with lining up in twos, finding partners, etc. (and whether there was a partner for me!). And yet when the children were counting out numbers of multilink, they spontaneously talked about whether their number was odd or even (I didn't even mention it!). I did then ask what they thought odd and even meant, and they explained in terms of pairing and two equal groups and one odd one left over on its own… It was an amazing understanding for five- and six-year-olds with no formal teaching at all on the subject. I suppose I am aware now of the requirements in the National Curriculum for odds/evens and so I'd brought the children's attention to it in everyday routines, but I hadn't planned to focus on it until next term.'

Being aware of what you are trying to develop in mathematics allows you to build it into children's experiences naturally. This leads to the best learning of all.

The potential for mathematics within children's everyday school lives is enormous and can make huge economies in learning time. If children can begin to understand odds and evens by lining up for assembly or dinner in pairs, then you will not need to spend so long pairing up numbers of cubes later on. Children learn mathematics best when it is as closely related to their own experiences as possible. It has to be *active*. Whether they are engaged in practical work and discussion, mental imagery, problem solving or pure mathematical investigation, their minds must be actively engaged in mathematical thinking (e.g. deciding, discussion and reasoning). This happens naturally when children are in control of their learning, and can be seen especially clearly when they are involved in free play. Active mathematical thinking is happening already, constantly, as children go about their daily lives, making sense of the world around them.

'One sometimes hears that "Mathematics is all around us". This is not accurate: mathematics is in people's minds, a kind of knowledge which can be used in many different ways to understand and organise what is around us.'

(Skemp, 1989)

Infant teachers have always seized opportunities during the school day to focus upon real, relevant mathematics where it naturally occurs. For example, the sorting and comparison of sizes and shapes involved in tidying up might be commented on:

- 'I can see you're sorting the curved and straight bricks.'
- 'Do you think all those are going to fit in there?'
- 'Which ones are you going to put in first?'

The ever-ingenious infant teacher might make the whole tidying up experience into a counting and timing game (e.g. 'How many do you think we can count to before it's all done?'). A minute or three-minute sandtimer might be set, giving them a real feeling for the passage of time in standard units. The mathematics that is built in or naturally occurring in children's everyday school lives usually 'just happens' or is 'a bit extra'. But it is worthy of a much higher status than this. Especially for Key Stage 1 children (though I don't see why it shouldn't become a focus in all Key Stages), this incidental mathematics can be planned for and developed into an explicit part of the curriculum.

The pressures of the National Curriculum have temporarily pushed aside some of the spontaneous fun we had with mathematics (and other curriculum areas) during the school day. It is time to bring it back and demonstrate its worthiness. Mathematics in children's everyday activities has always been, and still is, a tremendously powerful way of engaging children in Using and Applying. Many of these experiences, by occurring regularly, can develop so that children's mathematical thinking is constantly challenged. For example, sending children out to play in groups according to certain criteria can start to include quite complex classifications and mathematical ideas. (The first few times may simply involve 'the set of children who are six' or 'who are wearing white socks'. The game can build to 'the set of children who are six, who are *not* wearing white socks *and* who like peas' so that children have to think hard about whether they fulfil all the criteria. See page 61).

When I began teaching infants, I used a published scheme of workcards for mathematics which neither I nor the children were ever particularly excited about. We did them dutifully and the children seemed to progress well enough. But I have always liked mathematics and seen it within or built it into all the other things that went on in the classroom. I have also always believed in children deciding and thinking things out for themselves. Looking back now, I think the children in my classes learned about mathematics from the 'hidden' mathematics curriculum, which was driven by Using and Applying, rather than from their workcards, which were not.

The presence of Using and Applying is forcing us to bring the mathematics curriculum closer and closer to children's own ideas and experiences. The 'hidden' mathematics curriculum is already there.

Each chapter in this section is considered for its strengths in terms of the National Curriculum Programmes of Study for Mathematics, although there are often opportunities for focusing on other areas of the curriculum as well.

CHAPTER 3

CLASS PROJECTS

This chapter includes:
- Making huge models
- Organising real events
- Solving real problems
- Making displays and decorations
- Making class books
- Creating special areas
- Conclusion

You may sometimes work with the whole class to make or do something that benefits everyone (perhaps connected to your topic), for example: making huge models; organising real events; solving real problems; making displays and decorations; making class books, posters, etc.; creating special areas.

Generally, the more you can involve the children themselves in the decision making, the more actively involved and motivated they will be in the whole project, including any mathematics that is required.

MAKING HUGE MODELS

Figure 3.1 shows ideas of the sort of huge models you might have made in the past (or might still make under a Design and Technology heading). The home corner might become a café, or a pillar might become the mast of a ship ... The most exciting ideas for children are often the ones they can get inside or interact with. You only need to use boxes and fairly inexpensive materials (e.g. chicken wire, old boards and posts, string, papier mâché, corrugated card, old pieces of furniture). If the children are doing all the deciding, collecting, planning or making between them, then this doesn't require so much of your out-of-school time. First, the children should be involved in deciding what to make, perhaps from some suggestions that would all link to a topic or serve some other objectives, e.g. a topic on journeys

FIGURE 3.1

(a bus, boat or plane), a topic on money (a shop, restaurant or bank), something to help children to talk and create stories (a hollow tree, a fairy-tale cottage). A simple vote will involve counting and checking:

- 'How many of you prefer to make a cottage? a castle? a cave?'
- 'Does that all add up to the number of children here?'
- 'Let's check it again, between the castle and the cave.'

After deciding what to make and where it's to go, the children can each do some designs for it. This time the voting of whose design to use could involve ballot papers which certain children can be in charge of collecting, checking, counting and presenting the results to the others. Of course, they may not have chosen *your* favourite design: 'I had a fixed idea in my head that the castle would be grey, but Shelley's design was made of coloured stones – pinks, purples, blues, greens … That's what we had to make, and I must admit it does look good!'

Aspects of the Programme of Study so far:

- Collect, record and interpret data arising from an area of interest (Data handling);
- Begin to check answers in different ways;
- Count orally up to 10 and beyond (Number);
- Use a variety of forms of mathematical presentation (Using and Applying).

Parts of the job of making the model should be allocated to various children so that everyone is involved at some stage (allowing as much choice as possible). The mathematical focus becomes measuring (getting a feel for appropriate sizes) in scaling up from the original design:

- 'How big will the window need to be?'
- 'How much paper will we need to cover ...?'
- 'How much glue? Will this be enough?'
- 'How big should we do the leaves? or wheels?'
- 'If they're doing the legs, we need to know if our boots will fit.'
- 'How high should the door be for us to get in?'
- 'Where should the controls go so we can reach them?'
- 'How long will the sign need to be?'

From the Programme of Study, children are:

- using purposeful contexts for measuring;
- comparing objects, using appropriate language, by direct comparison, choosing units (if necessary) and estimating (Measuring);
- developing different mathematical approaches and looking for ways to overcome difficulties (Using and Applying).

Finally, there will be a focus on solving problems:

- 'How can we make the door open and close?'
- 'How can we fix the steering wheel on?'
- 'Does it matter if the colours are different?'
- 'What could we use for the sail? How big?'

Many aspects of the Programme of Study for Using and Applying will be involved.

In summary, the main mathematical strengths of making huge models will be Data Handling, Measuring and Problem Solving. These strengths lie in the collective making of the model. Of course, you may decide to *use* the model for something mathematical too (e.g. deciding on a type of shop so that children will be handling money, or designing a robot that can calculate).

ORGANISING REAL EVENTS

Some ideas for the types of event that children can be involved in planning are shown in figure 3.2.

In planning and organising the food for their Christmas party, a Key Stage 1 class suggested the things they'd like to have:

FIGURE 3.2 *Real events that children can be involved in planning*

- cakes
- ice-cream
- crisps
- jelly
- sandwiches
- biscuits and ...
- ... a bar of chocolate!

We don't usually put out a bar of chocolate (or two) to share at a party, but why not? (This idea was accepted and the chocolate purchased, after two children had worked out what size bar was best and how many bars would be needed for everyone to have two pieces each.) A group of four children chose to plan and prepare the sandwiches. This involved giving everyone a small piece of paper to draw their favourite type of sandwich (their idea), but then they couldn't remember what all the drawings were in terms of fillings. However, having got an idea of the types of fillings most people had said they liked, they then designed their own data-collection sheet to find out how many sandwiches to do for each of three favourite fillings. They then worked out how much bread to buy.

The number work required in the slices of bread problem was quite a challenge. They had one loaf of sliced bread to look at and the knowledge that there were twenty-four children to cater for.

Simon   Do we count the crusts or not?
Chris   Yes ... twenty, twenty-one, twenty-two slices! *(More than he'd thought.)*

Simon If it were two more, it would be twenty-four. *(The number in the class.)*
Roy We need more bread.
Teacher How many sandwiches will this loaf make if we put two slices together to make a sandwich?
Chris I think twenty-one. *(Only those two slices together?)*
Simon I think thirteen.
Roy I think eleven because I counted them.
Teacher What did you do?
Roy I counted in twos.

FIGURE 3.3

The children were then left on their own at a table (with the loaf of bread and pieces of paper) to work out how much bread they'd need. They knew now that one loaf of twenty-two slices would do eleven sandwiches, but how many more sandwiches did they need?

Richard It might be eleven more.
Chris How are we going to do it?
Simon If we had a robot ...
Chris I'll get a calculator.

At this point, they spent about ten minutes 'playing' with the calculators before they returned to the task (reassuring themselves and helping each other to make them work for additions).

Chris 11 + 22 ... no ... 11 + 9, 11 + 5, 11 +15, 11 + 14, 11 + 13. Yes! We need thirteen more sandwiches!
Roy So how many slices of bread?
Simon How can you do *that* on a calculator?

Richard went off to get the unifix to make some 'sandwiches' and did thirteen of them. Then he counted twenty-six 'slices'.

Roy   Twenty-two slices in a bag ... So we need three loaves ... *(smiling)* You don't need a calculator for that. It's quicker in my head.

Richard   And Mrs Barrows can have the rest for her tea!

The Programmes of Study for Number and Using and Applying are very much in evidence. The group were:

- choosing a suitable method of computation, using apparatus where appropriate, or a calculator;
- using (addition) to solve problems with whole numbers;
- counting in steps of two;
- developing flexible methods of working with number, orally and mentally;
- discussing their work, responding to and asking mathematical questions;
- developing different mathematical approaches and looking for ways to overcome difficulties;
- selecting and using the appropriate mathematics and materials.

But there is more than all this. They were developing new understandings about the 'basics' in mathematics (addition, doubling and halving) in a context that was real and for a purpose. They remained engaged by the task because they actually had to go and buy the bread and make the sandwiches. They *needed* to know how much to buy for real, not to answer some hypothetical teacher-devised or text-book problem. It is also interesting to note how they quite naturally chose to use mental methods (whenever possible) and a calculator or equipment (whenever necessary). They didn't use the pencil-and-paper methods they'd been taught (though they did write down in their own way how they'd worked it out afterwards).

Data handling and number work were also strongly in evidence when pairs and groups of children were organising the biscuits, crisps, cakes, drinks, party games, prizes and balloons.

Organising a Teddy Bears' Picnic or a tea party for parents and toddlers is very similar to the Christmas Party in terms of mathematics. Planning a visit out of school, however, can also involve routes and approximate times. Even very young children can take a part in such things (e.g. for a walk to the local park, there may be several possible routes from school which the children can discuss and represent in 'picture maps' on paper. Is the quickest way the most interesting? About how long would the longest way take?). Organising plays, performances, concerts, assemblies, etc. will involve decisions about how many people can be in the audience, where they can sit, finding out who can come, etc. It is always worth considering how much of this planning you can adapt to include the children as mathematicians. For example, Hannah was used to being involved in the planning of class assemblies and came to school one day with an idea that everyone liked. She said she'd been playing with her Noah's Ark and imagined all of the class coming into the hall two by two with animal masks on. We decided to do it! The children themselves organised how many different animals would be needed, which ones, who would like to be what, what they would do in terms of songs, stories, how many things they would have time to do, etc.

Sports Days offer opportunities for children to organise in advance who would like to do which two races, how many of each race will be necessary, what races to offer, new 'fun' races to invent, who will do what on the day (e.g. putting chairs out, recording results, offering drinks of water, etc.).

A very simple event that could be organised by pairs of children at any time is providing drinks of water (or orange juice) at playtime in the summer (see page 116). All you need is some empty plastic bottles and some plastic or paper cups. The children must decide themselves how much they will need, how many cups, how much in each cup, whether to include children from other classes, etc.

The main mathematical strengths of organising events will be Data Handling, Number and Problem Solving. These strengths lie in the organisation and planning of the event, but you could also make the event itself something mathematical (e.g. a maths games library, a maths evening for parents, a maths assembly, etc.).

SOLVING REAL PROBLEMS

Instead of nagging at the children or becoming increasingly frustrated, try using the types of problems in figure 3.4 to focus on some of the thinking skills necessary in Using and Applying mathematics, e.g. testing and checking ideas, refining, adapting, reflecting.

1 Identify the problem.
2 Choose a possible solution.
3 Evaluate how well it works.
4 Refine it, adapt it or try something else as necessary.

FIGURE 3.4 *Real problems that children can be involved in solving*

In identifying the problem, you may need to gather some information about what is actually happening, what might be causing it. Ask the children what they think and consider conducting surveys to find out more. For the playtime problem:

- 'What don't people like about it?'
- 'How many times do people fall over?'
- 'Why? Is it always the youngest ones?'
- 'How often are they knocked down?'
- 'How often are children coming in and out of the building? What for? Which classes are they from?'

If the children do conduct surveys over a period of time, they should be encouraged to decide the following for themselves as far as possible:

- 'What shall we study?'
- 'How will we collect the information?'
- 'How shall we organise and present our findings to the class?'

These provide an opportunity within the Programme of Study to 'collect, record and interpret data arising from area of interest' and to 'use a variety of forms of mathematical presentation'. The choice of a possible solution to the problem will arise after discussing and interpreting the information gathered and listening to each other's ideas. Don't be too steered by your own views on the best solution, because if the children are genuinely able to try out their ideas, they might make them work out of sheer motivation and determination!

The solution itself could involve mathematics. For example, in trying to stop the arguments about whose turn it was next on the computer, or on the cushions/chairs, or for tidying up, some children could devise a rota that would be fair and agreed to by everyone. This might involve:

- making lists, grids, tables;
- working out numbers of children per session and how many sessions before you have your next turn.

If they devise a rota that doesn't work, it will soon become apparent, and they can rethink it themselves. It is important to let things go wrong sometimes and share in helping them to put it right, instead of stepping in beforehand to tell them or lead them to see why it won't work. For example, one group organised a rota and completely forgot to put themselves in it! They were pleased to see the rota working over several days before they realised! The class agreed that they could all have two goes each to compensate.

Children will be more attentive to their own thinking and working if they know that it really is up to them. Like walking across a log, they are much more able to balance themselves without you standing just beside them ready to catch them all the time should they stumble! We mustn't be over-protective in our children's thinking and learning if we want them to become more independent.

Evaluating how well the solution is working can be quick and easy if the problem is solved (temporarily at least) or partly solved and some refinements and adjustments can be made. If the ideas didn't work at all, then you need to consider why (e.g. was the problem caused by something else?) and what to try next. You can always add your own ideas to the discussion and ask the children what they think, but be aware that imposing your own solutions will take the thinking and learning out of the task.

Devising rotas can involve:

- using an increasing range of charts, diagrams, tables (Data Handling);
- counting and checking,
- recording in a variety of ways (Number);
- developing different mathematical approaches and looking for ways to overcome difficulties,
- discussing their work, responding to and asking mathematical questions (Using and Applying).

Generally, solving real problems has the following strengths in terms of mathematics: Number, Data Handling and Problem Solving.

MAKING DISPLAYS AND DECORATIONS

When I began teaching, I spent ridiculous amounts of time after the children, the other staff and even the caretaker had gone home, preparing and putting up displays of children's work and creating an inviting and stimulating (I hoped) classroom environment. My biggest aim was to engage the children's surprise, pleasure, interest and intellect when they came into school the next day. I was pleased when they exclaimed, 'Ooh! Look what Mrs Lewis has done!' and became involved in the display. What a fool I was. It took me several years to realise what was wrong. I was wearing myself out being imaginative and creative on their behalf, instead of letting them be imaginative and creative themselves. I found it difficult to relinquish this aspect of teaching because I personally loved art, design and lettering; but I began to use the children's designs instead of my own for any outlines of animals, people, giants, buildings, etc. We all knew in our class that it was Adam's ferocious wolf on the wall, even if it looked a bit like a cat to any visitors! Children began to haul their parents in to 'Look at *our* Peter and the Wolf!') Then I began to let the children do some of our displays themselves, in groups, in classtime, and I became more of a facilitator, who was much more deeply excited by the real achievements of the children.

In designing and making displays in the classroom, the children are using and applying a huge amount of mathematics (mostly Shape, Space and Measures). The types of displays and decorations that they can be directly involved in include those shown in figure 3.5.

FIGURE 3.5 *Displays and decorations*

Even putting the backing paper onto a board can involve mathematics:

- 'How much paper will we need?'
- 'Is this piece about the right size?'
- 'I'll cut a shape to fit that gap.'
- 'We mustn't overlap too much.'
- 'Try turning that piece around … '

(You will need to consider safety for your own class. If the boards are too high, can some tables be securely set to stand on? Should you use drawing pins? Could you lay the correct size down on the floor in sheets of newspaper sellotaped together? Can some children cope with being given the measurements?)

In mounting their own work, the children will be measuring in a variety of ways to ensure that their mount is just a bit bigger than their work all the way round. There will be a lot of estimation and trial and error:

- 'I think this piece will be about right.'
- 'Oh, no! I cut too much off … Now I'll have to cut a bit more off this side.'
- 'I'm going to use a pencil and ruler.'
- 'I'm going to fold it first.'

Don't trim their mounts for them afterwards if they are satisfied with them. Why spend ages trying to measure and cut in a straight line if your teacher just trims it later?

Paper chains are worthy of a special mention, as they offer a wealth of opportunity for:

- length ('How long does it need to be?' 'Is it as tall as me yet?' 'Let's join ours together.' 'Will it stretch across the room?');
- number ('Ours are the same length – have we got the same number of links?' 'How many links to go across the room?');
- repeated patterns ('My pattern goes red, green, gold; red, green, gold … ' 'What's next? What colour will your tenth link be?');
- investigation ('What's the longest paper chain you can make from one sheet of A4 paper?');
- problem solving ('Can you make a mini paper chain to fit across this Christmas card?').

Almost anything for display can involve mathematics if you can step back from your normal role and think about how much of it the children could do for themselves. The mathematical strengths of the children making displays and decorations are Measuring (especially length and area), Shape and Space, and Using and Applying.

FIGURE 3.6

Aspects of the Programme of Study that are likely to be involved are:

- using purposeful contexts for measuring,
- comparing objects: using appropriate language, by direct comparison, and then using common non-standard and standard units of length; choosing units appropriate to a situation, estimating with these units (Measuring);
- describing and discussing shapes and patterns,
- recognising and using the geometrical features of shapes,
- describing positions, using common words,
- recognising right angles (Shape and Space);
- selecting and using appropriate mathematics,
- selecting and using mathematical equipment and materials,
- developing different mathematical approaches and looking for ways to overcome difficulties,
- understanding the language of number; properties of shapes and comparatives,
- discussing their work,
- asking questions, including 'What would happen if …?' (Using and Applying).

MAKING CLASS BOOKS

FIGURE 3.7

Class books, posters, letters, newspapers, etc. are often an excellent way to involve children in writing for a purpose (figure 3.7). But the making of these things, in terms of sizes, shapes and layout, also offers an excellent way to involve children in mathematics for a purpose. Think about how much of the designing and making could involve pairs or groups of children.

Why not all of it? You could discuss, make suggestions and share ideas about:

- what paper to use (e.g. colour, thickness, texture);
- what shapes and sizes;
- how many pages;
- how it could be special or different.

There will be experimentation, trial and error, new ideas to try, decisions to make and several real problems for the children to solve, many of which will involve mathematics:

- 'How can we make a pop-up page or a lift-the-flap book? What about peep-through holes in pages?'
- 'If we use letters of this size, will the headline or title fit across the page? Where should the first letter go?'
- 'Which sized pictures can fit where? Will there still be enough room for the writing?'
- 'If we fold large sheets of paper into a book, which pages will be next to which other pages?'
- 'How can we fasten pages together? Will any of the space on the page be lost into the binding?'
- 'What features of real books, posters, newspapers, etc. could we incorporate? How?'
- 'Who will do what? When? How long do we need?'

Only you can decide when and how much of the decision making can be handed over to the children, depending on your priorities and time available. The children's involvement can range from just two children being given the task of designing, writing and photocopying a letter to parents (for the class) to a huge class project of creating a class newspaper over several weeks, involving everyone (an excellent account of such a project with Year 2 children is reported in *Child Education*, January 1995, pages 29 to 34).

Aspects of the Programme of Study that are likely to be involved:

- describing and discussing shapes and patterns,
- describing positions, using common words (Shape and Space);
- comparing objects and events using appropriate language,
- using purposeful contexts for measuring (Measuring);
- collecting, recording and interpreting data arising from an area of interest (Data Handling);
- asking questions, including 'What would happen if ...?',
- selecting and using the appropriate mathematics,
- developing different mathematical approaches and looking for ways to overcome difficulties,
- organising and checking their work (Using and Applying).

Unless there is an emphasis on numbering the pages of the book (or newspaper) or on costings, there is unlikely to be very much number work. However, in one class, the children all had to use half a piece of uncut sugar paper for the pages of a class book and were seen to be doing this in a variety of ways (from folding to measuring with metre rules). The teacher drew everyone's attention to all these ways of halving and asked for any other ways to do it.

In the discussion that followed, the children were led to think about:

- what a half really is (i.e. does it have to be only that way round? Yes in this context, but not normally);
- halving of numbers of centimetres (different strategies for doing so);
- accuracy (i.e. did it matter if you'd only guessed? What if your line wasn't straight?);
- checking (i.e. were the two pieces the same?).

So it is always possible that something from the Programme of Study for Number will arise!

The mathematical strengths, however, of this type of activity are Shape and Space, Measuring and Problem Solving.

CREATING SPECIAL AREAS

Many schools decide to create a special area in the school building or grounds at some time (figure 3.8).

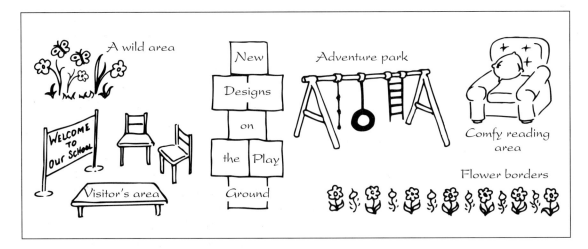

FIGURE 3.8 *Special areas*

Before doing so, think about how much Key Stage 1 children can be involved. Try not to decide on everything in the staffroom. The children themselves can be imaginative and helpful in their designs and ideas. The most obvious area to involve mathematics is in creating new designs to be painted on the playground. Children can take turns to use chalk to do number targets, squares, ladders, etc. and try them out before painting begins (figure 3.9). Key Stage 1 children can certainly be involved in designing the shapes, sizes and numbers, whilst older Key Stage 1 children (or other parents and helpers) set about the painting itself. (A very long number snake was painted on one playground, twisting all over the tarmac with numbers up to 165. Unfortunately, there was a mistake in the numbering which the children themselves found later. But they loved this missed-out 'mistake' number (76) and invented many games based upon it, e.g. '76 you sink, you're out', 'You have to do an extra jump here for 76', 'Jump in twos, watch out for the secret trap door!' Children love the surprise of irregularity in mathematics, as if they can play with its structure and regularity, being in control of it. It may be worth making a deliberate mistake in your playground design, though genuine mistakes are best!)

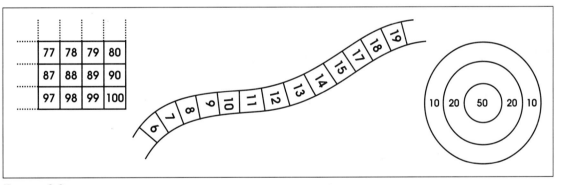

FIGURE 3.9

In chalking designs onto the playground, young children will often do them too small to use effectively. They will obtain a very real feeling for scale and size as they try to draw the same design much larger next time. Judgements about distances will also be necessary if small pieces of PE equipment, such as bean bags, balls and quoits, are to be used in conjunction with the designs.

The designing of any area will most probably involve Shape and Space and Measurement. The designing of flower beds and borders can also involve repeated patterns. It sometimes helps to provide modelling equipment to explore possibilities (e.g. plasticine 'soil' to stick coloured beads for 'flowers' on, or used matchsticks to make possible fencing arrangements for a proposed 'wild area').

The main mathematical strengths, therefore, of creating special areas are Shape and Space, Measurement and Problem Solving.

CONCLUSION

When young children are genuinely involved in the decision making about real things that affect them directly in the classroom, they will be learning:

- to develop problem-solving strategies (e.g. the first strand in particular of the Programme of Study for Using and Applying Mathematics);
- to use and apply (variously) ideas of Number, Data Handling, Shape and Space, and Measures in a variety of contexts;
- to develop personal qualities (e.g. perseverance, motivation, confidence) in relation to mathematics.

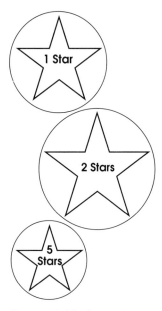

FIGURE 3.10 *Star coins*

Sometimes children will be satisfied with an outcome that you wouldn't be. As far as possible, their reasoning and ideas should stand, although this doesn't mean that you can't offer your ideas and suggestions alongside theirs. For example, when one class were suggesting ideas for a class shop, it was the teacher's rather late suggestion of a magic shop (selling spells, spiders, broomsticks, tricks, etc.) that everyone liked best. But the children argued for magic money to pay for things instead of the real 1p, 2p and 5p coins that they usually used (and which was the main mathematical reason for having a class shop). So a compromise was reached, and the magic money was made – but it was based on our decimal money system. The children made one-star, two-star and five-star coins (figure 3.10).

Later on, some of the older children made ten-star, twenty-star and fifty-star coins, as well as a one-moon coin (equivalent to a hundred stars). In making their magic money, the children actually studied the system of real coins in great detail and had to make decisions about how many of each coin they were likely to need. And they still had all the calculating practice later on in paying for goods and giving change.

EVERYDAY ACTIVITIES

This chapter includes:
- Register time
- Collecting money
- The structure of the day
- Assemblies
- Birthdays
- Going out to play
- News time
- Getting changed
- Getting into groups
- Lining up
- Library
- Playing/Choosing
- Singing
- Cooking
- Tidying up
- Story time
- Home time
- Conclusion

A Key Stage 1 classroom is full of routines and activities that eat into the planned curriculum time. Listening to young children's news, getting changed for PE or simply tidying up can take ages. There is potential for mathematics (and for other curriculum areas no doubt) to occur spontaneously *and* to be planned within these everyday routines and activities. A question or a comment, an idea or an activity that is offered during these times can help children to see the mathematics that they are using and challenge them to think mathematically.

The ideas offered here are starting points for you to dip into, try out, adapt and build on. You probably do a lot of these things already, and more besides. But the mathematics is so directly and immediately relevant to the children's experiences that it is worth actively and explicitly developing as part of your scheme of work.

'… the successful teachers built on children's everyday experiences …'

(OFSTED, 1993)

REGISTER TIME

'Taking the register' is normally done as quickly as possible, twice a day, before the 'real' learning time begins. Children are expected to sit still, answer to their name and do nothing for the rest of the time. Then, a child is often chosen to take the register to the school secretary. So where's the mathematics in that? Children may be vaguely aware of the order in which the names occur (e.g. 'I'm always near the beginning, I'm always after Yvonne') but this isn't made explicit. The following table offers some ideas for register time.

Questions/ideas	Mathematics
'Can you say your own names, in order?' It takes even less time to do the register (sometimes it's hard to keep up with them!) and the children are concentrating on who's before and after them, with everyone helping as it progresses. (It usually only takes two or three attempts before the class can do this without your help.) It is very clear when someone's away, as the flow of names comes to an abrupt halt for a second whilst the absence is noted, and can then continue as before. Beware! Other children may say the name of the absentee inadvertently, trying to help the order to progress. Be sure you hear each child's own voice!	• Order and sequence
'Can you say your names in reverse order?' Once they are confident with the order of names, ask them to concentrate on making the list go backwards.	• Order, sequence and inverses
'How many children are in our class? How many are absent? So how many must be sitting on this carpet? How do you know? How did you do it? How could we check?' The repetition of these same questions over several days soon builds confidence in handling the numbers involved and draws attention to different ways of checking (e.g. calculators, counting).	• Mental calculation and checking
'How many children for school dinners today? For sandwiches? Going home for lunch?' *'How can we be sure everyone has a turn at taking the register to the secretary?'* Test and discuss their ideas.	• Problem solving

Questions/ideas	Mathematics
'Would anyone like to fill in the register for me today with my pen?' Year 2 can cope well with this, and everyone loves to see the teacher on the carpet!	• Data handling • Using tables and grids to record information
'Whilst X goes (walking so beautifully!) to take the register to the secretary, how many do you think we could count to before he/she comes back?' Much fun can be had with this if you deliberately speed up or slow down the counting to make the estimates just right each time! 'How are you all so good at estimating?! What's happening? It's always a different estimate each day and it's always just right!' (Teacher looking very surprised!)	• Estimation and counting

I tried some of these variations with one of my classes. After a few register sessions where children called their own names in order, we tried speeding it up each time until eventually they could do it faster than I could mark the little dashes into the book! Kevin then suggested that we tried it just saying 'Yes' instead of names. It was amazing that thirty young children could concentrate together, listen for their turn and complete such a task, at speed, without error. I began to long for someone to be absent, so I could catch up in the moment it took for someone to say 'Sian's away'!

COLLECTING MONEY

Money is frequently collected and counted in school. Even if dinner money is no longer collected at the beginning of each week (one teacher told me that she used to do almost all her mathematics from the dinner money, but now it is sent straight to the secretary), there will probably be:

- trip money;
- collection of real 1p and 2p coins for the class shop;
- tuck-shop money;
- charity collections;
- raffle tickets or sponsorship money.

Children will learn far more from handling and counting real money than working with the artificial plastic kind. Are larger coins always worth more? If a smaller coin is worth more, then is it made from the same metal? Is it the same thickness? Does the shape change? (Figure 4.1.)

FIGURE 4.1

Are foreign currencies made up in the same way? Don't be afraid to ask these sorts of questions without knowing the answers yourself. Children need to know that they can genuinely investigate systems and structures alongside adults, and that adults don't always know the answer.

Questions to keep them thinking whilst you open, check and count all the dinner money (or trip money) on a Monday morning are offered in the following table.

Questions/ideas	Mathematics
How much do you think will be in here? Let's count it and see …	• Prediction based on experience
What's this coin? What's this one? Which is worth more? So why is this one smaller? That's strange …	• Recognition of real coins
What shape is this envelope? Is it still an oblong this way round? What about this way?	• Shape
I wonder what coin we'll have most of this week?' Pile same-value coins on top of each other to make towers that children can see growing higher.	• Prediction
Choose two towers where the tallest one *doesn't* have most coins(e.g. £1 coins are thicker): *This is the tallest tower, so do you think it will have most coins? Let's see …*	• Data handling 'Graph' with real coins
When counting, try deliberately counting with no fixed rhythm and ask children to watch carefully and only count when a coin is picked up/put down. This helps children who can recite number names in order to realise that they need to match one name to one object when counting.	• Counting and one-to-one matching
Oh dear! How much is this? Too much or too little? How much change do we need to find? Or How many days might this be for? How could we find out?	• Calculation and problem solving
Who would like to have a go at adding up, or recording, all the money/coins we've got here today? You can use a calculator, pencil and paper, whatever you think might help. Don't forget to check somehow …	• Calculation and checking

Even if dinner money is sent directly to the school secretary, it is worth considering sending two children each time to help to count it up and check it. Don't be afraid of the numbers being too large, the secretary and/or calculator will help as much as necessary.

These suggestions are not intended to make every register time and dinner-money time last half the morning and generate lists of mathematics questions to plough through, but it is possible to inject a little mathematics into such times, often without increasing the time spent. Because it is a regularly occurring event, small mathematical ideas can build and grow over the term, until children become more confident and fluent with the mathematics involved.

THE STRUCTURE/ORDER OF THE DAY

Some aspects of the school day are fixed (e.g. we take our coats off when we arrive, lunch time is always at 12 o'clock, etc.) whilst others are more changeable (e.g. storytime could be before lunch today, assembly will be this afternoon). From time to time, it's useful to get children to think about the structure and sequence of their day.

Questions/ideas	Mathematics
What's first when you arrive at school? What things do we always do first? (e.g. coats off, go to the toilet, wash hands, look at picture books, etc.)	• Order
Can you be even more detailed? (e.g. open the door, walk to my peg, put my bag down, take my coat off, hang it up, say goodbye to Mummy, etc.)	• Sequence of events
Can you be even more detailed??! (e.g. lift my hand up, press the handle down, push the door, etc.)	• Precision of language (describing position and movement)
Stop everyone! In a few minutes, we have to do something else. What do you think is next? Are you sure? How do you know? What will be after that?	• Prediction based on experience • Justification
What's generally the sequence of our day? Can it be described in just three parts? (e.g. 'come to school, work, go home'; 'morning, lunchtime, afternoon'.)	• Sequence of events • Early ideas of division

Questions/ideas	Mathematics
Can you describe it in lots of parts? What sorts of things would you say if you had to describe it in a hundred parts!?	
Would it matter if we changed the order of our day? (e.g. tidying up first, lunch time last, storytime first, playtime last.) *What matters? What doesn't matter? Why? Let's try changing something for fun. What shall we change that doesn't matter?*	• Developing reasoning (e.g. 'What would happen if...?')
We only have five minutes before going home. Shall we sing a song or play our number game? *We have half an hour for our assembly. That's like two playtimes!*	• Ideas of the passage of time (in standard units)

Sometimes it's worth agreeing on three (or more) jobs or activities that the children can do in any order, deciding for themselves. It will foster independence and motivation if they have some control over their tasks.

ASSEMBLIES

Which way do the children face in your assemblies? Could they turn the other way round? Do they sit in rows or in horse-shoes and circles? Do you play music whilst the children walk in and get settled? Most of the ideas below are based upon whole school assemblies.

Questions/ideas	Mathematics
How many chairs do we need for the teachers and other adults? Who could put them out and watch to see if there are enough or too many?	• Counting • One-to-one matching
How much music do you think we'll need whilst everyone is coming in and going out? A whole cassette? One side? A few songs? Who could be in charge of the music today and find out?	• Estimating (time) • Measuring time (amount of cassette used)
Try marking a semicircle with chalk (on the hall floor) that would be just the right size for our class to sit around.	• Estimation (length)
Make it larger or smaller next time if necessary.	• Improving an estimate on the basis of experience

Questions/ideas	Mathematics
Try marking a line in chalk across the hall to show where each class should sit. Is there enough room for each class? Do the older children need more space?	• Estimation (area of floor space)
Is there an order to which class sits where? Why? Could the younger children sit on chairs behind the older ones?	• Order of size
Is there an order to which class leads the assembly? Who will be next? How long will it be until our turn?	• Sequence in time
Have a quiz after assembly – just a few questions to see if the children noticed things, e.g. *What did Mrs Banks have on the table? About how many children were at the front?* After a while, get the children themselves to invent the questions. (Remind them about the quiz before assembly!)	• Not specially mathematical, but useful anyway

There are often problems associated with the running of assemblies (e.g. noise, fidgeting, not starting on time, taking too long, not suitable for all ages, etc.). Try getting the children themselves to evaluate these factors and to suggest improvements (see page 41 for the possible mathematics involved). Of course, the assemblies themselves can sometimes have a mathematical focus (see page 124).

DATE, CALENDAR AND WEATHER

A few minutes each day to focus on the time, date, calendar and weather can reap huge long-term mathematical benefits, often related to number work.

Questions/ideas	Mathematics
Include the time (digital and analogue form) as well as the day, date and year. Record it.	• Telling the time
After discussing the weather, go back to check the time, day, date and year. The time will have changed, but the others stay the same. *How many minutes have passed?*	• The passage of time • Mental calculation
Sometimes have another look at the recorded time, day, date and year much later on. *What's changed now?* (Hours as well as minutes.) *Don't the other things ever change? When will they change?*	• Units of measurement of time

Questions/ideas	Mathematics
Are there always seven days in a week? thirty-one days in a month? four weeks in a month? twelve months in a year? (Especially when you are near the end of a week, month or year.)	• The structure of days, weeks and months
How many days until …? since …? (Especially useful in December during advent, but good for any event.) *How did you work it out? How did you know?*	• Calculation • Methods of calculation
What's the number in the date today? Try writing it in the air, on your hand, on the carpet, on someone's back …	• Writing numerals
What will the number be tomorrow? the next day? next week? What was it yesterday? the day before?	• Sequence of numbers (ordinal number)
Whose turn is it to do the weather chart? (Perhaps following register sequence.) *Which picture/word best describes the weather today?*	• Using a chart • Using symbols
How many people agree/disagree?	• Comparing numbers of children (more/fewer)

If you have a calendar that requires filling in (e.g. a commercially produced wooden board with numbers, days and months on 'tablets'), it's fun to play 'spot the mistake' where you (and later the children can take turns to do this) deliberately make a mistake for them to find. 'Mistakes' can range from the wrong day or date or month to something that is back to front, upside down, in the wrong place or missing. Get the children to use words to describe how to put it right and deliberately misunderstand them wherever possible in order to get them to become more precise with their mathematical language!

Another game to play is to set the calendar at a date that they would like it to be (e.g. Christmas, birthday, a Sunday) which often involves interesting discussions and checking about the correct day.

Advent calendars are worthy of a special mention because of their enormous potential for mathematics. A huge class advent calendar can be designed and made by the children themselves (with all the Measurement, Shape and Space and Using and Applying that is involved (see pages 43–6)). In opening the doors each day, there is the problem to solve of everyone having a turn (e.g. twenty-eight children and only twenty-four doors) and also what to do about Saturdays, Sundays and the days after the end of term. There are daily mental calculations to be made about how many days until the end of term and how many days until Christmas. The calculations can be done in different ways and checked in different ways each day. There is a constant visual reminder on the wall of number complements to twenty-four (e.g six doors open, eighteen days left to Christmas Eve). At the beginning or end of each week, there is the opportunity to add or subtract three to each number. This is all extra to the basic recognition of number symbols to twenty-four and finding them, in order.

FIGURE 4.2
Advent calendar design

FIGURE 4.3

One class designed their advent calendar on quarters of circles after having worked on halves and quarters for a few weeks. They made six circles with 'quarter doors' (figure 4.3).

As the numbered quarter doors were removed, they were kept and reassembled into circles as the days progressed (figure 4.4).

The children were constantly fascinated by the quarters, halves, three-quarters and wholes of the circles, both of the pictures and of the removed doors. They particularly liked seeing half a circle as shown in figure 4.5.

FIGURE 4.4   FIGURE 4.5

BIRTHDAYS

Birthdays are extremely important to Key Stage 1 children and provide the opportunity to think about time and numbers.

Questions/ideas	Mathematics
How old are you? *How old were you yesterday/today/tomorrow? last week/this week/next week? last year/this year/next year?*	• Passage of time
How old is your sister/brother/friend? *How old will they be when you are …?*	• Mental calculation
Will you ever catch them up? Can you ever be the same age? Why?	• 'Same' difference
Count the correct number of candles and the correct number of claps for each birthday person. Does it matter how fast or slow the claps are?	• Counting
Make a 'half cake' and set the task for older (more able) children to find their 'half-birthday' using calendars and calculators. (You could organise a day of halves on someone's half birthday (see page 121).)	• Solving numerical problems
What are babies' ages measured in? *How many months old are you?* *How could you find out?*	• Solving numerical problems
Are people who are older always taller?	• Developing mathematical reasoning

Whenever it's someone's birthday, it can be fun for them to be given their age in claps, very quietly at first and getting ready for a huge, loud clap at the end. Young children will concentrate hard on the order of numbers, anticipating the moment when they can do the big clap, getting a feeling for how near they are to the final number. The value of such simple activities cannot be overestimated. (Don't forget to let them do the claps for your birthday too, and any helpers or pets!)

GOING OUT TO PLAY

Instead of the hustle and bustle of everyone going out to play at the same time (causing commotion in the cloakroom), mathematics can readily be used to organise the procedure:

Questions/ideas	Mathematics
Send the children off in groups or sets, according to various criteria. Start with one criterion, e.g. *Everyone wearing black shoes. Everyone who is six. Everyone who has a dog at home.*	• Defining a set
Put two criteria together, e.g. *Everyone with lace-up shoes and wearing a vest. Everyone who is five and has short hair.*	• Using two criteria together
Introduce what's not in a set, e.g. *Everyone who is not seven. Everyone who does not have a baby brother or sister.*	• What's not in a set
Use increasingly complex combinations of the properties of each set of children, e.g. *Everyone who likes ice-cream, who isn't smiling and who is wearing white socks.* (Children will be concentrating hard to work out whether they match the requirements!)	• Developing mathematical reasoning
Comment on the sizes of each set or group of children as they go.	• Counting or comparing
Deliberately make some sets very large or small, and sometimes include impossible 'empty' sets, e.g. *Everyone with a pet monkey. Everyone who is older than ten.*	• The 'empty' set
Make sets that include the whole class, e.g. *Everyone who is in this class. Everyone who is sitting on the carpet.*	• The universal set
Let the children take turns to define the sets (they will think hard about criteria that enable their friends to go first!).	• Choosing criteria
If you want them all out quickly, challenge a child to choose criteria that will include large groups of children.	• Developing mathematical reasoning
Try sending them out in reverse order from the register (i.e. youngest first). See if they can do it themselves, without any help from you.	• Order and sequence (inverse)
Set challenges for groups of children to walk off to play in certain ways, e.g. backwards, sideways, turning, low down, stretching tall, making themselves as wide (or as narrow) as possible as they go, in a curved path or in straight lines like a robot, using large steps or as many tiny steps as they can, etc.	• Using language of measures and movement

The criteria game for sending children out to play in groups must start simply and build gradually over many days/weeks/months into the more complex combinations of criteria. A new idea, challenge or surprise can be introduced whenever it feels right to you. Only you can know how to pace this game so that everyone continues to be involved and surprised by it. The main thing is that it should just be a bit of fun (if someone is looking fed up, then send out the set of children who feel fed up!) with some highly worthwhile mathematical undertones.

Of course, playtime itself can be the subject of mathematical ideas if children are involved in:

- designing number tracks and targets for the playground (see page 49);
- creating rotas for the use of small pieces of PE equipment (see page 43);
- conducting surveys about playtime problems (see page 41);
- using playtime and the playground as a resource for work on mathematics (see page 136);
- creating ideas for games and things to do (see page 69);
- providing a playtime drink or snack (see page 116);
- lining up in classes to come back in (see page 65).

NEWS TIME

News time is typically unpredictable about what spontaneous opportunities for mathematics (or other curricular areas) may occur. We can never know when someone is going to turn up with a huge icicle (for which the children can predict how long it will take to melt and how much water there will be), a new toy to look at (for which they can try to describe how it works or moves) or simply with the news that they went swimming with their Grandpa (for which they might talk about how deep the pool was, e.g. 'the water came up to here on me and only to here on Grandpa when we were standing up!'). But whatever the news is, there are some things we can do to increase the learning potential of such times.

Questions/ideas	Mathematics
After a few moments of looking at something, hide the item behind your back and ask the children some simple questions about what they might have noticed, e.g. *What colour were the eyes? How many wheels were there? What number was at the end?* (If you do this often, then the children start to really look and listen, noticing lots of details whenever anyone shows anything or says anything. The become very attentive and enjoy it as a game of memory.)	<ul><li>Counting</li><li>Observing and remembering numbers, shapes and colours</li><li>Using mathematical language</li><li>Searching for properties</li></ul>

Questions/ideas	Mathematics
Tell a friend first and then let the friend report back to the class (this helps to get to the 'essence' of the news more efficiently and can help some children to talk).	• Developing language and communication (sometimes mathematical)
What do you think … is going to tell us about? e.g. What are the clues? How do you know? or Why can't we know?	• Prediction based on varying degrees of evidence or experience
How many children would like to show us or tell us something? About how long can each child have? (Can some wait until tomorrow or until playtime, if necessary?)	• Counting • Early ideas of division

GETTING CHANGED

Young children can notoriously take a long time to get changed for PE, dancing, swimming or simply getting coats on ready to go home. Mathematical ideas can speed them up a bit and provide a learning experience at the same time.

Questions/ideas	Mathematics
How long does it take for everyone to get ready?	• Timing in minutes or Counting
How long until the first person is ready? *What if we help each other in twos?*	• Predicting
Who will be ready first, second, third, fourth? (Right up to the thirty-first and last, if possible.)	• Ordinal number
As soon as you are ready, find whoever is least ready and help them. *How many helpers can we get each time?*	• Counting
What's the maximum number of helpers possible? *Why?* *What's the minimum number of helpers?* *How could that happen?*	• Mental calculation • Developing mathematical reasoning
Get changed in mixed-age groups. *Which group will be ready first (and tidiest)?*	• Ordinal number
Does the larger group get ready more quickly, more slowly or the same as a smaller group? *Why?*	• Reasoning

It can be useful to do the timing by counting aloud, with children joining in when they are ready. Give yourselves a number target for each time the children get changed. Involve the children in estimating how long it will take them. 'Freeze' the counting (and the children stop like statues) from time to time in order to see how everyone's getting on and to remind them about helping others.

If you are timing in minutes, let the children take turns to do the timing in various ways:

- sand timers, recording how many times the one-minute, three-minute or five-minute timer was turned and then calculating the total;
- stop watches and stop clocks (if available and suitable for Key Stage 1 children);
- the class clock or wrist-watches, recording the time (in their own way) at the start and at the finish and then trying to calculate the difference. (Digital watches will lend themselves very well to the task becoming a calculation problem.)

Calculating the time taken might be possible to do mentally together hearing how a few people did it, or might have to wait until later when some children can settle to try to work it out in their own way.

GETTING INTO GROUPS

It is often necessary to organise the class into groups, e.g. for working, for PE, for country dancing, for sports, for planning a party, for tidying up … Wherever possible, it is best to give various children the task of organising the groups beforehand, as this provides a real purpose for mathematics.

Questions/ideas	Mathematics
When children organise groups beforehand: *How many children are there in total? How many groups do we need?* and/or *How many children need to be in each group? Does it matter who's in which group: Can it be random? Is it fair? Are all the groups to be the same size?*	• Solving number problems
When groups are organised on the spot, instead of doing the calculations yourself for how many children need to be in each group, or how many groups you will have, ask the children to estimate and then try out their ideas.	• Estimation (of number) • Trial and adjustment

Questions/ideas	Mathematics
If we start with these four as group leaders, about how many will we have in each group? Let's try it … *How can we make sure that all the groups are the same size with no children left over?* *This group is huge and this one tiny.* *About how many extra children does the large group have? Will the groups be the same size if we transfer those extra children to the smaller group? How many should we transfer?*	• Mental calculation • Solving numerical problems • Number differences

LINING UP

If children line up in twos, then an opportunity for talking about odds and evens arises. If there are several lines of children (e.g. classes lining up to come in from playtime), then it's possible to highlight number differences.

If children simply make one, long line, then a focus on ordinal number can arise.

Questions/ideas	Mathematics
Try making two lines according to certain criteria, e.g. boys/girls, fives/sixes, before and after someone on register, likes … /doesn't like … Do they ever match? How many more/fewer each time? (The children will have to pair up first.) *How many shall we move over from this line so that they are both the same?*	• Number differences • Mental calculation
Line up in twos and find out if there's an odd one out or an even number of children. Emphasise the number of children as an odd or even number.	• Odds and evens
Chalk and then paint a number snake along the corridor or edge of classroom (wherever the children line up). Children can each stand on a number. When it's time to go: • count (whisper) the numbers as you tread on them; • send first all the children who are standing on a number, e.g. with a three in it, bigger than twelve, smaller than seven, whose digits add up to four, that is odd/even (with help), that is only made of straight lines, whose digits are the same, with a zero, one or two in it, etc.;	 • Counting (saying number names in order) • Properties of numbers

Questions/ideas	Mathematics

• *go when you've tapped the floor that many times;*
• *the third person can go. What number were you on?*
  Now the ninth person ... second ... sixth ... eighteenth ...
  (Match aloud to the number they were on each time.)
	• Counting
	• Ordinal number

For several lines of children (e.g. teams or classes): first people in each line touch fingers; second people in each line touch fingers; third people in each line touch fingers; and so on until you get to the end of one class and can see the number differences emerging. Send the number differences in first, then first row, second row, etc.	• Ordinal number • Number differences

LIBRARY

Using the class 'picture-book area', reading corner or the school library has many possibilities for Shape, Measures and Classification.

Questions/ideas	Mathematics
Organising and tidying. *Check that all the tickets are back in the library books.* *How many are missing?* *How many books are being borrowed at the moment?* *Can you put this pile of mixed-up books back in the correct places?* *Can you check the shelves?* *Can you sort out the reading scheme books?*	• One-to-one matching • Counting • Sorting and classifying • Ordinal number
Which way does this book go on the shelf? *Describe it so that I can put it back properly. I'll do exactly what you say. Is this what you mean? Like this?* *Where does it go?* *Which way round?* *Which way up?* *Facing which way?* (Deliberately get it ridiculously wrong until they are more precise!)	• Describe position and movement • Developing mathematical language
Design and make some 'pockets' to keep each person's library ticket in.	• Measures • Problem solving • Shape

Questions/ideas	Mathematics
Organise a system for borrowing books, e.g. Where to put returned books? How many can be borrowed? For how long? Try it out. Improve it as necessary.	• Problem solving
Is every page numbered? Find some unnumbered pages. What numbers should they be? (This can be interesting for pages before page 1.)	• Ordinal number
Which do you think is our biggest book? Is it bigger than any other book in height, width, thickness, number of pages, number of words ...? How is it bigger?	• Language of comparison in measures
Take these reference books back to the school library and find the correct place for them (look at the books' numbers or codes).	• Using a classification system

Picture books can also be used as practical equipment for measuring and data handling.

PLAYING/CHOOSING

Children in free play should not always be left completely alone. Neither should teacher intervention take the initiative away from them by imposing tasks, however gently. It doesn't matter if your input is not acted upon. Children must know that they do not have to take up your suggestions; that your ideas are genuinely offered alongside theirs as no more than extra thoughts. Many play activities are, of course, naturally mathematical. For example, whilst freely playing, children are likely to be immersed in the following mathematics:

Sand and water	Exploration of measures, especially volume and capacity
Home corner	Early number work, measures and sorting
Construction toys	Using and applying ideas about shape and size
Puzzles and games	Mathematical reasoning, often using shape and numbers
Painting/Printing/Junk modelling	Using and applying ideas about shape and size
Plasticine/Clay/Playdoh	Creating and exploring shapes and sizes
Pretend shopping	Counting and calculating

Questions/ideas	Mathematics
Sand and Water Children can take turns to empty and refill the water tray whenever it is necessary to do so. *How can they do it without spilling any? How much water is there? How long does it take? What would they like to put in (e.g. a few drops of food colouring, bubbles, cubes that need a wash, plasticine, play people, cooking equipment from the home corner)?*	• Problem solving • Volume, time and capacity • Quantities and sizes
Use stones, wood, toy buildings, etc., for children to create landscapes, routes and pathways in the sand tray.	• Language of position and movement
Play with size: Have mini sand and water trays with tiny containers (e.g. thimbles, acorn shells, pen tops, etc.). Choose only long items (e.g. sticks, old paintbrushes, pieces of string, etc.). Choose only heavy items (children to decide what counts as heavy). Will everything sink?	• Exploring measures
Set some impossible challenges: • *Can you make a hole in the water?* • *Can you make a slope/hill of water?* • *Can you make dry sand into a bridge? They'll find a way!*	• Creative thinking • Investigating • Trial and error
Home corner *Make a pretend meal on a plate for the home corner using cubes, cuisenaire, counters, plasticine, etc. Work out how many of everything you will need to do three more plates the same. Go and get exactly the quantities you think you need and see if you were right.*	• Calculating and checking
Have a pretend doctor's visit to the home corner: • *Do a prescription (How many tablets or spoonfuls of medicine? How often? For how many days?)* • *Bandage up a limb (How long should the bandage be? Which size to choose?)* • *Choose an appropriate sized plaster for a wound* (perhaps painted on with face paints). • *Take a pulse. (How many beats per minute?)*	• Number • Size and shape • Counting and time
Add old suitcases and holdalls for packing (folding, fitting clothes and items into the shape and volume of the cases).	• Shape and size

Questions/ideas	Mathematics
Children can arrange simple wild flowers (or garden flowers) in a vase for the home corner. They should choose an appropriate size vase and cut stems to different lengths for an interesting display. *How much water should go in the vase so that the level is just right after the flowers have been put in? Why does the water-level change?*	• Length and height • Volume and capacity
Construction kits (These include lego, wooden bricks, polydrons, clixi, mini-quadro, octons, etc.) Mix a construction kit with: • toy cars (to make car parks, garages, roadways); • little figures (to make furniture, houses, play parks); • animals (to make zoos, farms, safari parks)	• Making judgements about sizes and shapes
Have a 'take it apart' (or 'repair') table (e.g. old gadgets, radios, watches, and models that children have made and that are ready to be taken apart and put away): *How many parts do you think there will be? How many of these? This is a funny shape! How would you describe it? Is this the same shape as this? How? Why? Is it still a circle with all those little 'teeth' around it?* The bits can be sorted afterwards and put away if necessary, or else used to add details to junk models and collages.	• Number • Shape • Sorting
If the children have already made: • a tall construction – *How tall is it possible to make it so that it still stands up? What shape would be most stable?* • a long construction – *What if you used all the pieces? How long would it be then? What if you turned some pieces around another way?* • a person, vehicle or animal – *Can you make something for it e.g. a bed, a friend, a bridge, an enclosure, a baby …*	• Measures and shape • Estimation and exploration of length • Comparing of measures • Problem-solving
Puzzles and Games (These include jigsaws, boardgames, tangram puzzles, verbal games, outdoor games, etc.) Change the rules and adapt games: • *It's over already! How could you change the rules to make it last longer?* • *Can you make it work for two players instead? (or three or four …)* • *Can the game be played backwards? How?* • *What would happen if you started at 100 instead?* • *Choose your least favourite game or puzzle. Change it to make it really good.*	• Mathematical reasoning • Trial and error • Predicting

Questions/ideas	Mathematics
Have an 'invent your own' box with any loose pieces, a few dice and counters, a calculator, pieces of cardboard and pencils. Add something new from time to time (e.g. a few plastic spiders or some shiny buttons). Let the children invent games, testing them, adapting them and testing again, writing down the rules or teaching someone else how to play. You may need to emphasise the need to keep them fairly simple! If a game works well they could make a box for it and design a cover.	• Number • Reasoning • Mathematical communication • Shape and measures
Puzzles: *Which way up does it go? Does it matter? Why?* *Could it be done upside down?* *Could you fit that piece in with your eyes closed?* *Tell me how to put the next piece in. I'll do exactly what you say …*	• Shape and space
Children can make their own puzzles by cutting number squares or shapes into pieces. They could try making double-sided puzzles by colouring a picture on both sides of the cardboard before cutting into pieces.	• Problem-solving
Painting, Printing and Junk Modelling *Imagine that your model is upside down. What shapes would you see? Try it, if possible. What does it look like from underneath?* *Imagine that your printing pattern could continue off the page. What would be about here? And here? About where would the next leafy shape be after this one?*	• Shape and space • Estimation
Compare two paintings: *Who's got the largest piece of paper? Who's painted the largest thing? Is the smallest picture also the smallest thing in reality?* Add a box of assorted bits and pieces beside the painting, printing and modelling areas (e.g. scraps of gold and silver foil or material, tinsel, old buttons, bits of wire, wool, polystyrene pieces, string, twigs, seeds, anything!)	• Exploring relationships between sizes • Exploration of shapes and sizes
Printing: *Let me see … I wonder which thing you used to get that print? Was it …? That's funny. An oblong print from a plastic tree shape?!!? How?* *What if you printed on another side? What shape would you get?*	• Shape and space • Prediction

Questions/ideas	Mathematics
Plasticine, Clay, Playdoh ... *What's happening to your playdoh?* (As it is moulded, rolled, squashed, stretched, cut, etc.) *Is it changing shape, or size, or both? How? Is there more or less of it now that it's thinner and longer?* *Could it be changed back again? (Don't do it unless you can easily and want to.)* *Would it be able to stretch/reach right across the board/table? What about across the room?* ('No, silly!' said Jane, 'but maybe if it was very, very, very thin!') *Which model is heavier?* *Would it be heavier if they were real? (e.g. a big, fat, juicy, worm and a tiny model house).*	• Language of shape and size • Conservation • Prediction • Exploring mass
Make a set of numerals that: • *each balance their own number of conkers (or grams)* • *each measure their own number of cubes in height (or centimetres)* • *are made up of their own numbers of parts/pieces*	• Mass • Length • Number
Shopping Have real coins in the tin or till. The children can keep a record of how many there are of each coin at the beginning and end of each session. (Only have 1p and 2p coins if you prefer. The children can collect these over time.)	• Recognition of coins • Counting • Checking
Let the children organise: • Pricing (have a sale or price increases from time to time e.g. everything costs 2p more) • Stocktaking (making lists of stock and quantities, 'ordering' new items as necessary.) • Advertising (making paper bags, signs and posters) • Opening and closing times (include a clock or watch for the shopkeeper) • Receipts (so that items can be returned and money refunded) • Arranging the stock (e.g. larger items at the back so that customers can see everything) • A 'total liquidation' sale where 'everything must go' before changing to another type of shop or café, or ice-cream van, or fairground stall.	• Reading and writing prices • Calculating • Data handling • Checking • Shape, space and measure • Time • Calculation • Checking • Shape, space and measures • Calculation • Reading, writing and negotiating prices

Involve the children in organising play activities. (How many children at each activity at any one time? How can everything be set up and tidied away properly?) Let them know that if they have any ideas for making surprising or interesting changes to the play activities, they should say so.

SINGING

Quite apart from all the obvious number songs, the singing itself can be full of repeating and growing patterns that can be made explicit to children. There are also opportunities for addition and subtraction.

Questions/ideas	Mathematics
Change the numbers in various songs, e.g. start at a higher (or lower) number. Carry on singing if possible, using higher (or lower) numbers. Increase or decrease by more than one for each verse. (Seven green bottles … and if three green bottles should accidentally fall …)	• Ordinal number • Mental calculation
Do something different on the third (or any number) verse, e.g. whisper it, stand up for it, mime it. (Children anticipate where the special verse will be, getting a feeling for the place of that number in the sequence of counting numbers.)	• Ordinal number
Highlight the pattern of verse, chorus, verse, chorus. Do something different on alternate verses to create repeated patterns: • loud, soft, loud, soft • two people, everyone, two people, everyone • sitting, standing, sitting, standing	• Repeated patterns
Highlight the growing (or shrinking) pattern of songs that increase (or decrease), e.g. ten men went to mow, nine men … eight … Make them increase or decrease by two each time, starting from different numbers. Make them increase or decrease in loudness.	• Number sequences • Number patterns
Find different ways to mime the actions to various number songs, using objects and the children themselves. Try progressively taking away the singing each time until only actions are left (like 'In a cottage in a wood').	• Representing (modelling) a calculation or a number pattern in different ways

Questions/ideas	Mathematics
Singing 'in a round', e.g. 'London's Burning', where the second group start singing when the first group are halfway through. It never ends!	• Repeating pattern • Idea of infinity
Add clapping rhythms to songs. Try to describe them in words.	• Repeated pattern

Changing the numbers in songs is particularly good for developing a mental agility with numbers in children. If they already know the song well, then they will have a mental picture of the things involved and can enjoy 'playing' with the numbers.

On a recent school trip in the coach, we started singing some number songs. We'd already changed a few names and numbers for fun when Ruth suggested that we sing 'Five little ducks went swimming one day' starting with 100 ducks! We had a good go at it, but most people got fed up and exhausted by the time we'd got down to seventy-five ducks. Ruth and her friend, however, continued (on and off) throughout the day until they got to the end! Of course, no Mother Duck would have 100 ducklings, so the song could have been adapted to 'ten Mother ducks said "quack, quack, quack"' (perhaps say ten quacks!) and the number of ducklings could decrease by ten each time.

COOKING

Questions/ideas	Mathematics
Organise a rota for who, when, how many people each time, how many sessions, etc. (Children should work it out and record it in their own way.)	• Problem solving
Collect and count any money involved. Have shopping expeditions for small groups of children. Find out how much things cost on a first visit. Work out what to buy and how much it will cost altogether (in their own way, in school). Buy items and check change. Use calculators and real coins as necessary.	• Counting • Calculating • Recognition of coins • Solving real numerical problems
Create their own survey to find out what most people would prefer to make and eat. (Offer some suggestions first.)	• Data handling
Try cooking for a tuck shop at playtime, which would involve more counting of money and giving change (homemade biscuits only need to cost 1p or 2p each).	• Counting • Calculating

The opportunities for mathematics above are all extra to what is involved in the cooking itself:

- measuring quantities;
- counting (numbers of biscuits, numbers of spoonfuls, etc.);
- measuring time;
- shapes (cutters, 'balls' of dough, etc.);
- estimating sizes and quantities;
- conservation of quantities.

It can be difficult to know just how much of the mathematics young children will be capable of when cooking or shopping, and it is easy to underestimate them. The hardest things are (often) to allow sufficient time for them to work on relatively simple problems, and to recognise that the small parts they can play in more complex problems are highly valuable in themselves. In adding up the costs of items on a real shopping list, you may think that a younger child can't cope and exclude them from that part of the activity. But they could learn so much from perhaps:

- adding up the pounds only, leaving the pence to someone else;
- finding the keys to press on a calculator to do it;
- adding just two items;
- doing the 'rough estimate' to check.

For example, for the biscuits we were making for the school fête, Lyndsay volunteered to work out how much we would earn from forty-eight biscuits if we sold them for 2p each. It took her a whole session to get to an answer that she was happy with and had checked! This delayed my planning considerably, but I shall never forget her concentration and counting, sitting in front of rows and rows of pairs of counters.

TIDYING UP

Tidying up can be subject to the same kind of timing exercises as for getting changed (see page 63) and could also involve the mathematics of creating rotas (see page 43) (e.g. for who does what, where, who with and for how long). Apart from this, the tidying up itself has mathematics within it.

Questions/ideas	Mathematics
Packing bricks, construction sets, cubes, etc. back into their containers. *Will all those really fit in there?* *Does it matter how they're packed?* *Try packing them as closely as possible.* (The pieces might need sorting first.)	• Volume • Shape and space
Washing and replacing paint brushes, glue spreaders, etc. *How many of each kind should there be?* *Are any missing? How many?* *How do you know?*	• Counting • Matching • Calculating
Putting crayons and pencils back into pots. *Which ones go where?* Ask children to: distribute mixed crayons evenly amongst pots; sort out thick/thin, short/long, etc. as appropriate; tidy the paper trays, putting larger sheets underneath and sorting into types of paper (e.g. thickness).	• Sorting • Counting • Sharing • Comparing • Area • Thickness
Ask the children to find ways to label storage areas so that even the youngest children can put things back properly (e.g. outlines or silhouettes of the objects, draw pictures/diagrams and/or write labels, use old catalogues to cut up, take photographs).	• Representation (towards symbols) • Measuring (for correct-sized labels)
What would it be like if some things were not sorted or tidied, or else sorted in an inappropriate way? Deliberately mix something up. Does it matter? Are some things better mixed up (e.g. assortment of crayons)?	• Developing mathematical reasoning

Tidying many areas of the classroom will require some sorting and comparing, often including numbers of things.

STORY TIME

Predicting, estimating and reasoning feature very strongly at story time.

Questions/ideas	Mathematics
What do you think is going to happen? Why? *What do you think now?* *Can you tell from the pictures?*	• Predicting based on experience
How many do you think there are? About? *Could it be twenty, fifty, 1000 …?!* *Could it be two, five, zero …?!* Count and stop halfway to revise estimates if necessary.	• Estimating (numbers)
Could that really happen? Why? Why not? *Would the same thing happen if …?*	• Developing reasoning
About how big/small would he/she/it be if he were in our classroom?	• Estimating (size)

Many stories have mathematical themes too (see page 88).

HOME TIME

Questions/ideas	Mathematics
What time do we need to start getting ready to go home (given that it usually takes us ten minutes)? *What would a digital watch say for that time?*	• Telling the time • Calculating
What do we do? In what order?	• Sequencing
Which is quicker, buttons, zips or poppers when putting on coats? Predict first. Split into groups to find out, roughly. Send slowest group first next day.	• Order • Prediction and testing
This group try to find your coat pegs with your eyes closed. *How did you do it? Describe the route.* *Or* *Go blindfolded to the door.* *Use words to describe how to move to get to the door* *(e.g. three steps forward. Stop. Turn to the left).*	• Language of position and movement
A letter for everyone to take home: *How many do we need?* (Excluding people whose brother or sister will have one.)	• Mental calculation

Questions/ideas	Mathematics
How many do you think are here? Let's count them to check. (Count unrhythmically, making sure one number name is said for each letter.) Or *Here's some for you to count, and some for you, and you…* (Write down how many each person had and add them up together, sharing methods of calculation.) *Will we have any left over? How many?*	• Counting • Calculating methods

You could also suggest something to do on the way home occasionally, to involve mathematics.

Questions/ideas	Mathematics
Everyone look for and remember the biggest number they can find. (Where was it? What was it?)	• Number search
In a car (or bus) or walking holding hands with an adult. *Close your eyes and count to ten or twenty. Before opening them try to guess where you are. How close were you?*	• Estimating and imagining distances and routes
Look for squares, patterns, clocks. (Whatever fits in with your mathematics theme.) *What did you find? Where?*	• Applying mathematics to the real world
Count how many left or right turns. *Is it the same for everyone? Did anyone get home without a left or right turn?! Is it possible?*	• Turning (left and right), quarter turns
Do the people who live nearest to school get home the quickest? *How could we find out? What would we need to know?* (Could be measured very simply by what's on TV as soon as they're home) (Depends on cars, stopping to talk, calling in somewhere, waiting for buses, etc.)	• Developing mathematical reasoning
Who arrives back at school first, second, third, etc.? Sign in as you arrive. Does the order ever change? How much? How often? (Could put the next number against their name as they arrive, or simply pick up the next number and keep it till everyone's together.)	• Ordinal number

CONCLUSION

The mathematics that has emerged most strongly throughout these ideas is:

- Mental Calculation (and Calculation Methods);
- Counting to find out how many;
- Ordinal Number;
- Problem Solving, Prediction and Reasoning;
- Measures (especially time);
- Shape, Position and Movement;
- Data Handling.

I was particularly surprised, in totting up how often each type of mathematics occurred, to find so many references to number work (especially calculation). The Programme of Study for number specifies giving pupils opportunities to:

- develop flexible methods of working with number, orally and mentally;
- use a variety of practical resources and contexts.

And, of course, they must also have opportunities to:

- use and apply mathematics in practical tasks, in real-life problems and within mathematics itself;
- explain their thinking to support the development of their reasoning.

These opportunities can be provided, in part at least, through children's everyday activities. But in order to make use of them you will need to:

- not worry about levels (most ideas are open-ended enough for the child to respond at their own level);
- not worry about outcomes (children will find their own answers, which may not be yours);
- not worry about progression as a strict linear hierarchy (in challenging children to think for themselves, they will be forging ahead themselves in their learning);
- not worry if things go wrong or are not responded to (real-life mathematics is bound to have some times like this. Expect it, learn from it, laugh about it);
- not be afraid to ask questions of children for fun (look surprised, challenge correct answers, 'Why?', 'Is it really?', 'Are you sure?!', etc.) This helps young children to become more confident in their knowledge and understanding of mathematics and to know that they are to think for themselves.

Sometimes these ideas for mathematics from everyday activities can spill over into formal mathematics time (e.g. the calculation of amounts of money when shopping and cooking for real). In order to make room for this, you may need to let go of some of your more formal mathematics, allowing these ideas and others to mix in.

CHAPTER 5

OTHER AREAS OF THE CURRICULUM

This chapter includes:
- Science
- Geography
- Music
- English
- History
- Physical education
- Design and technology
- Information technology
- Art, craft and design
- Conclusion

'Mathematics is a powerful tool with great relevance to the real world. For this to be appreciated by pupils, they must have direct experience of using mathematics in a wide range of contexts throughout the curriculum.'

(Non-Statutory Guidance F1, 1989)

Children will be using mathematics in many different ways whilst working within other areas of the curriculum. From time to time, their attention needs to be drawn to this in order to make it explicit that they are doing some mathematics. It also makes sense for you to be aware of particularly strong mathematical experiences and opportunities within the other areas of the curriculum so that your scheme of work can be balanced and 'economies' made in terms of curriculum time.

There are some very strong overlaps sometimes between mathematics and other curriculum areas. For example, science and information technology involve large amounts of data handling. It would be foolish not to make use of this by cross referencing between the schemes of work for these subjects.

Topics have traditionally brought together different areas of the curriculum under a common theme and often help to provide purposes or contexts for children's activities. The mathematics that is planned through 'topic webs' can have more depth and meaning than the same curriculum work done in isolation. However, even greater benefits can be gained if we can plan some activities that naturally bring different areas of the curriculum together (e.g. research, experiments, displays, visits, etc.) instead of planning everything for the topic in individual subject compartments. Collecting information about the weather over several days, for example, may involve aspects of science, geography, English, mathematics and information technology at the same time. These kinds of activities can be extremely rich in learning. Even if we can't make every part of it explicit to the children, we can have a focus (or two) within an activity, based on its greatest strengths, and allow the other learning to happen as incidental and highly worthwhile extras. This is 'value-added learning'.

Mathematics can sometimes have a focus within work that is planned for other areas of the curriculum, whether within topics or not.

SCIENCE

Of all the subjects, science probably has the most overlap with mathematics. There are several elements of each of the Programmes of Study for science that are directly relevant to:

- Data handling;
- Measures;
- Using and Applying;
- Shape and Space.

Numbers will often be used, but do not usually become the focus of scientific activity, except where a numerical problem presents itself to be solved (e.g. in totalling and checking the tallies made in a survey).

In the Programme of Study for Experimental and Investigative Science, children are expected to:

- plan, predict and recognise when a test is fair (this is very like deciding and reasoning in Using and Applying mathematics);
- make and use measurements to obtain evidence (i.e. using purposeful contexts for Measuring);
- record results in drawings, diagrams, simple tables and charts (i.e. using a variety of forms of mathematical presentation (communication – Using and Applying) as well as aspects of Data Handling);

- consider evidence, make comparisons, draw conclusions and explain results (this will often involve mathematical reasoning and mathematical language and communication, i.e. Using and Applying).

Almost all of the mathematics outlined above would be involved in a scientific experiment such as finding out how the growth of broad beans is affected by light and dark. How can we be sure that everything else other than light and dark is kept the same? Should the seeds be planted at the same depth? Should we measure the amount of water used? How shall we measure the growth of the plants? When? How often? How shall we record the measurements so that they can be easily compared? What do we expect to happen? and so on. One activity, like this, can therefore help us to teach children about several aspects of mathematics and science at the same time. (It also, of course, involves the Programme of Study for Life Processes and Living Things.)

Life Processes and Living Things includes teaching children to look for similarities and differences between themselves and other pupils and to classify living things according to observable characteristics (Data Handling).

Materials and their Properties also requires some classification in sorting materials into groups according to their properties, recognising similarities and differences (Data Handling).
   Materials can also be:

- changed in shape by squashing, bending, twisting and stretching (discussing how the shape has changed helps to develop mathematical ideas about Shape);
- changed by heating and cooling (which may involve the vocabulary of measuring temperature – hot, warm, tepid, lukewarm, cold, freezing, etc.).

Physical Processes includes teaching children:

- to describe the movement of familiar things (e.g. cars getting faster, slowing down, changing direction) (which in turn helps children towards a mathematical understanding of position and movement, i.e. Shape and Space);
- that forces can change the direction and the shapes of objects (Shape and Space);
- that sounds travel away from sources, getting fainter as they do so (which may involve some comparison or measurement of distances).

The difficulty in planning for separate aspects of science and mathematics Programmes of Study is that it can be easy to miss these marvellously rich 'value-added' learning activities. For example, involving the children in feeding the birds on a regular basis could include the activities shown in figure 5.1.

• Making a bird table   (Science: Materials and their Properties
                              Mathematics: Measuring
                              Design and Technology)

• Making bird pudding   (Science: Materials and their Properties
  and other food and water   Mathematics: Shape and Measures)

• Making a hide   (Science: Materials and their Properties
                              Mathematics: Shape and Measures)

• Organising a rota   (Mathematics: Using and Applying;
                              solving numerical problems, data-handling)

• Setting up some experiments, including surveys
   (Science: Experimental and Investigative Science
                              Life Processes and Living Things
                              Materials and their Properties
                              Mathematics: Using and Applying;
                              Number, Data Handling, Shape, Space and Measures)

FIGURE 5.1 *Feeding the birds*

The main focus of feeding the birds might be Experimental and Investigative Science and Data Handling, once it is up and running and different children are finding out which birds use which kinds of food, when they come, how many of each kind of bird arrive, the effects of the weather, etc. But the 'value-added' extras outlined above make the whole activity highly efficient in terms of learning time, and every child, whatever their age or ability, can have a part in it. The data handling involved will be real and for a purpose – an experiment devised and controlled by the child.

GEOGRAPHY

There is a very strong relationship between geography and Shape and Space which it makes sense to exploit. There are also useful links with Measures, Data Handling and Using and Applying mathematics.

The Programme of Study includes teaching children to:

- follow directions, using much of the same vocabulary as for mathematical positions and movements: up, down, on, under, behind, in front of, near, far, left, right, etc. (Shape and Space);
- make maps and plans of real and imaginary places, using pictures and symbols, e.g. a pictorial map of a place featured in a story, a plan of their route from home to school. (Shape, Space and Measures);
- mark on a map approximately where they live and follow a route (Shape and Space).

In making and using maps and plans, children need to learn to match three-dimensional objects to two-dimensional images and vice versa. They also need to match images to symbols and vice versa. Activities designed to do this will, at the same time, be helping children to investigate the properties of three-dimensional and two-dimensional shapes and relationships between them. For example:

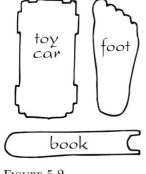

FIGURE 5.2

Draw round me

Draw round objects to see what shapes emerge e.g. toy car, foot, book. Try drawing the same object in many different ways. Use toy buildings to make a layout. Draw round them to make a plan. (N.B. Outlines are early symbols).

Silhouettes

Use an overhead projector to obtain outlines of shapes. Guess what the object is (e.g. pencil, cube, daisy, watch, drawing pin, coin, etc.).

Looking down

Imagine flying up near the ceiling and looking down. Fly over the top of something and draw what it looks like. We'll try to guess what it is … (e.g. a piece of Lego, pot of crayons, top of a bookcase) (figure 5.3).

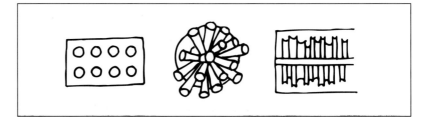

FIGURE 5.3

Simply drawing any picture will involve representing three-dimensional objects in two-dimensional form, but it's useful to challenge children to draw what the other side might look like (figure 5.4). (N.B. It is easier to do this first with a model or object that they can physically turn round or walk round and look down on.)

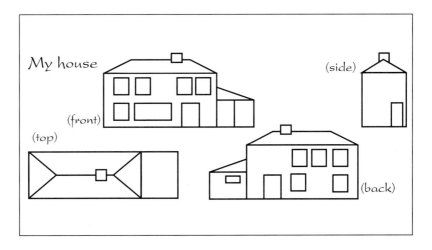

FIGURE 5.4 *Viewpoints*

The Programme of Study also states that in investigating places and a theme, pupils should be given opportunities to observe, question and record, and to communicate ideas and information. (The emphasis is on the children's own observations, their own questions and their own ideas, which is very similar to the ethos of Using and Applying mathematics.)

Other elements of the Programme of Study relating to places and themes will often require the children to collect information and will therefore provide the reason or purpose for Data Handling. For example:

- studying the locality of the school and distant contrasting locality;
- studying the quality of an environment;
- expressing likes and dislikes about places;
- looking at similarities and differences between localities;
- studying the effects of weather;
- studying how the environment is changing and how it could be improved.

Organising trails and treasure hunts, and using programmable toys will involve both mathematics and geography at the same time, through their focus upon routes, directions and distances.

MUSIC

Music provides an excellent and unusual context for the mathematical study of Repeated Patterns. It also involves several aspects of Measures and can help children to develop communication with symbols (Using and Applying mathematics).

The structure of songs and music often involves repeated patterns and 'growing' patterns (both algebraic ideas): songs and hymns can have choruses and refrains; music can be built up of a series of phrases to make a melody which is repeated; music can grow and diminish in loudness (dynamics). Discussing what repeats (and what nearly repeats!) in songs and music – helping children to recognise and to put into words (i.e. make explicit) what repeats – is all that is needed to draw the mathematics out of this area of the curriculum. For example, in 'Oranges and Lemons' there is the verse and the 'Here comes the chopper...' section that alternate throughout the game. Children might also notice the 'Chip Chop Chip Chop' repeated pattern, and you could extend this for several repeats before the final 'the last man's dead!'.

Number songs obviously overlap with mathematics for young children, helping with counting and visualising numbers of things. Growing or shrinking patterns are often in evidence as number songs progress (e.g. 'Five little speckled frogs ... four little speckled frogs ... three ...'). With some adapting, most number songs can involve larger numbers and/or mental calculation (e.g. Men going to mow a meadow in teams of ten: 'ten men went to mow ... ten men and their dogs, went to mow a meadow. Twenty men went to mow ... twenty, ten men and their dogs, went to mow a meadow'. Right up to 100 men ... 100, ninety, eighty, seventy, sixty, fifty, forty, thirty, twenty, ten men and their dogs, went to mow a meadow!) Let the children have their own ideas for changing the numbers in songs and try them out, even if they sometimes don't work. For example, Odelle suggested we sing 'Nine Hairy Monsters' with two monsters running away each time instead of one. We tried it and found that there was only one left at the end instead of two for the last verse! Lee said we should do two then one, two then one ... alternating to the end. The class was divided about whether they thought it would work. It did! We spent a little while puzzling over why ... (see also page 72 for number songs).

Apart from recognising the structure of music when performing, composing, listening and appraising, the Programme of Study also requires children to recognise and explore:

- pitch;
- duration;
- dynamics;
- tempo.

All of these can involve elements of measurement. Pitch can be compared as high or low, and much fun can be had by deliberately making it too high or too low when singing. Duration of notes can be long or short, measured by counting beats or clapping. Dynamics can be loud or quiet, measured by whether the sound can be heard (or simply by contrast within the piece). Tempo can be fast or slow, and can sometimes deliberately get faster or slower for effect. All of these things help children to develop a better understanding of comparison, using appropriate language and non-standard units, in measuring.

Music at Key Stage 1 requires that children use symbols to represent sounds. This often becomes quite mathematical, matching shapes, sizes and numbers to particular sounds, especially when children invent their own symbols which relate to various beats and claps, words, high and low notes, etc. (figure 5.5). It can be interesting, too, for children to try creating sounds and rhythms from each other's invented symbols, looking to see what they suggest to them.

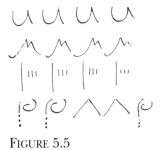

FIGURE 5.5

ENGLISH

There is a large overlap between English and mathematics because the vocabulary of mathematics is so important and because discussion is one of the most important ways in which to learn about mathematics.

The Programme of Study for Speaking and Listening includes giving children opportunities to talk for a range of purposes, including:

- exploring, developing and clarifying ideas;
- predicting outcomes and discussing possibilities;
- describing events, observations and experiences;
- making simple, clear explanations of choices;
- giving reasons for opinions and actions;
- exploring and discussing the meanings of words, their use and interpretation in different contexts.

All of these purposes can and should occur within a range of mathematical activities, especially if they are based upon Using and Applying.

Children are expected to participate as speakers and listeners in a group and also to ask and respond to questions. If children are doing these things in their English work, it can only help their ability to do so in Using and Applying mathematics.

The Programme of Study for Reading includes:

- making use of information sources, e.g. information technology-based reference materials (Data Handling);
- using stories, poems and chants containing patterned or predictable language (Repeated Patterns and Using and Applying);
- saying what might happen next in a story (Predicting based on evidence and experience) (Using and Applying);
- following the sequence of a story, e.g. when acting it out (Order of events).

There are many well-known stories and rhymes which are particularly relevant to mathematics (e.g. 'We're going on a bear hunt' has a strong repeated pattern and an inverse sequence in it). It would be useful, over time, to build up a list of stories (known to you and your class) under mathematical headings so that you can choose specific stories to support various mathematics themes throughout the year. Only include stories that naturally have a strong mathematical focus, and perhaps jot down any useful questions and ideas as they occur. For example, we had fun with *Anno's Counting Book* (Mitsumasa Anno, Macmillan 1975) by looking for examples of what *isn't* the number on each page (e.g. windows, bridges, etc.) as well as all the examples of each number. Some stories lend themselves well to adaptation to incorporate mathematical ideas; for example *Would you rather?* by John Burningham is good for inventing comparisons and choices:

- Would you rather ... have six twenty pence pieces or one pound coin?
- Would you rather ... have eight half-bars of chocolate or three whole bars?
- Would you rather ... run round the playground four times or run round the school field?

N.B. The children should invent some themselves, of course.

Number stories and rhymes can be adapted and changed (e.g. 'The Five Little Pigs' or 'Snow White and the Six Dwarves') so that children need to think afresh about the mathematical context of their new versions.

The Programme of Study for Writing includes:

- organising and presenting writing in different ways, suitable to purposes and audiences (including lists, captions, records and observations). This will help towards developing mathematical language and communication (Using and Applying);

- experimenting with spelling and discussing misapplied generalisations. (Talking about rules in spelling alongside their exceptions helps children to focus on general statements and related predictions in developing mathematical reasoning, i.e., Using and Applying).

Children making homemade books for their stories can lead to mathematical problems with numbers of pages. How often have you helped a child to staple or sew together a few pages of their book, only to find that the whole story is written and finished on the first one or two pages (leaving six or so pages blank for pictures)? Ask the children collectively for ideas to help to solve this problem:

- Think where half the story gets to...
- Write it on paper and cut it up to fit a bit on each page and glue it in.
- Make it a zig-zag book instead and cut it off when you've finished.
- Do the pictures first.

The problem is very likely to involve counting, fractions and judgements about the size (length and area) of the written text.

The Programme of Study for Handwriting includes:

- writing from left to right and from top to bottom of the page;
- starting and finishing letter shapes correctly;
- concentrating on the size and shape of letters;
- concentrating on the spacing of letters and words.

The language of Shape and Space will naturally be developed by this kind of work, as well as comparisons and judgements about size (Measures). For example, in talking about the shapes of letters:

- What's the same/different about them?
- How different can the same letter be and still be recognised?
- Can you describe the route in drawing a letter?
- Describe how to draw a letter without telling me what the letter is ... I'll see when I can guess ... Is this right? Is this what you mean?

English serves all areas of the curriculum and is, in turn, served by its use in other subjects. Mathematics is but one of many contexts and purposes to which English can be put. At the same time, mathematics *needs* English, especially in Key Stage 1, in order to function at all. Understanding the language of mathematics, discussing ideas and asking questions is absolutely fundamental to children's mathematical development. Some of this can occur, naturally, within your allotted curriculum time for English.

HISTORY

Studying history at Key Stage 1 will offer many opportunities for Data Handling and understanding time (Measures). There will also be opportunities to develop Reasoning (e.g. Why did most children walk to school?) in identifying similarities and differences between ways of life at different times.

In historical enquiry, children will be:

- finding out about aspects of the past from a range of sources of information;
- asking and answering questions about the past;
- communicating their findings.

These things will often include collecting, recording and interpreting information (Data Handling), and provide a real purpose for doing so. A class museum would also involve Data Handling if the children do the cataloguing, displays, calculating of ages and use of a computer database themselves. (A museum shop offers opportunities for mathematics, too. See pages 35, 71.)

The early stages of learning about history require an understanding of the passage of time. Children need to:

- sequence events and objects, in order to develop a sense of chronology;
- use common words and phrases relating to the passing of time, e.g. old, new, before, after, long ago, days of the week, months, years.

In doing so, children will be building the beginnings of a mathematical understanding of the measurement of time. Time-lines bring history and mathematics together, including aspects of ordinal number as well as measures. For example, start with a simple 'life-line' showing all the years of a child's life (figure 5.6). It could be concertinaed to help children to recognise the years (figure 5.7).

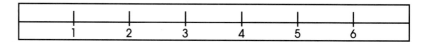

FIGURE 5.6 *Life-line*

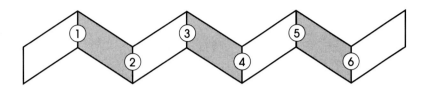

FIGURE 5.7 *Concertina time line*

The folds are birthdays. Children can draw pictures, write or stick photos onto each year as appropriate (with help from home) showing important events like moving house, starting school, special holidays, baby brother or sister being born, etc. An important mathematical point is that the time line does not have to be horizontal, or indeed straight, as long as the spacing between the years is consistent. Vertical 'life lines' can be easier to display. If they are made well, on good-quality card, they can be added to in both directions as the child reaches their next birthday (or simply thinks ahead to important events expected to happen in the future) and asks at home about things that happened before they were born, for example:

- How many years before I was born was my sister born?
- How far back does my time line need to go to when you were married?
- To when you were at school?
- To when you were born?
- How long would my line need to be to get back to when Granny was born?

If you make each year a foot long, then each inch can represent a month. (You may like to label time lines in years and challenge the children to find the month of their birthday for each year.) More mathematical interest can be created by making the same length of card represent a variety of different time periods. Some children could be:

- getting dressed and ready for school in sequence;
- a whole day from waking up to going to bed;
- a week of seven days;
- the academic year so far;
- the years of their lives;
- the last twenty years;
- longer periods of time as appropriate.

How big would each strip be if it had to fit into another strip's time scale?

PHYSICAL EDUCATION

Physical Education (PE) provides a marvellous context for the direct experience of Shape, Space and Measures. When children are inventing and creating movements and games for themselves, they will be Using and Applying these ideas.

Almost all shapes and movements can be made with the body, and many will occur naturally during the games, gymnastic activities and dance that you plan for the children. But because the mathematics is experienced so directly by each child, it is worth planning to make it explicit – drawing the children's attention to shapes, spaces, movements and sizes as they occur – and deliberately building in some mathematical ideas.

In the Programme of Study for Games, children will be experiencing how balls, hoops, quoits, bean bags, etc. move when they are thrown, struck, rolled or bounced. There is also an emphasis on the 'awareness of space'. Simple competitive games might involve pathways, specified movements and distances. For example, the children might set up their own obstacle course (or journey) in small groups, using an upturned bench as a bridge, quoits as stepping stones, ropes to show the path, mats as islands, cones as markers or trees, etc. They could:

- design it;
- decide on the rules for moving round it;
- test it out;
- race or time each other.

(They could also draw a map of it and describe the route.) Other games could be invented from given starting points, e.g. Balance a ball on a quoit. There are three bean bags with which to try to knock it off. Invent what happens next. Specific mathematical ideas can be built in by having certain restrictions or rules, e.g. the game must involve some turning or be based around a triangular shape or involve long distances.

The Programme of Study for Gymnastic activities includes teaching children to use a variety of movements (e.g. turning, rolling, using hands and feet, etc.) on the floor and on apparatus and to 'link a series of actions ... and repeat them'. Making repeated patterns or sequences of movement in PE lends itself to some excellent mathematical discussion:

- Can you work out what repeats in Leah's sequence? How many movements are repeated?
- Stop! What do you think is next?

- What part of the sequence do you think she'll be doing when she reaches us? Try it.
- Try repeating a different number of movements.
- How many repeats to take you across the hall? (Depends on the size of movements, the number of movements in each repeat, whether any movements take you backwards, etc.)
- Try doing your whole sequence backwards.
- Everyone start here and do five repeats. Where will you all end up? Try it and see.

Almost all the vocabulary of Shape, Space and Measures can be explored in the gymnastics lesson:

- Make yourselves long, tall, short, wide, thin, low down, flat, etc.
- Use up as much space and as little space as you can on the floor.
- Make yourselves move feeling very heavy or very light.
- Imagine the longest path you can to walk along.
- Go faster, faster, faster … slower, slower, very slow.
- Use huge steps, tiny steps.
- Turn your body through half turns, quarter turns, whole turns.
- Find a different way to turn your body (or body parts).
- Move in a straight line, curved line, circle, bigger circle, tiny circle, spiral, etc.
- With a partner, move over each other, under each other, behind each other, next to each other.
- In groups of three, make a triangular shape, a different triangular shape, another one …
- In groups of four make different-sized squares, oblongs, diamonds, etc.
- In pairs, let someone be the leader whilst the other pretends to be their reflection in the mirror.

For each of these simple starting points, it is likely that children will respond differently. Be alert to this, as it adds so much to the mathematical thinking. For example, in making triangular shapes, one group of three might use their feet as the vertices of imagined triangles, whilst another group might use their bodies (lying down) to be the sides/edges. One child could lie down whilst the other two lean together in an upright position, or children might even choose to make tiny triangles with their fingers or forearms. Actively look out for different ideas and prepare to be surprised!

The Programme of Study for Dance includes teaching children to perform movements or patterns and to use contrasts of speed, shape, direction and level.

The language used in these sessions is again likely to be highly mathematical. Traditional dances, such as folk dancing, country dancing, may-pole dancing, etc., will be full of patterns to explore and talk about. There will also be the need to organise children into twos, threes, fours or eights ... whatever the dance requires, all leading to practical discussions of: odds and evens; first, second, third couple to go; how far and how quickly to move to the music; what shapes to form, etc.

DESIGN AND TECHNOLOGY

FIGURE 5.8

The Programme of Study for Design and Technology actually specifies giving children opportunities to apply skills, knowledge and understanding from art, mathematics and science. Mathematics is integral to Design and Technology, especially in terms of:

- Shape and Space;
- Measures;
- Data Handling;
- Using and Applying.

The designing part of the process sometimes requires gathering some information from other people if the product concerns them, e.g. in designing a tuck shop for playtimes, children would need to have their own ideas and suggestions for contents – home-made biscuits, boxes of raisins, fruit, etc. – and then perhaps conduct a survey to find out how popular their different ideas would be.

The design of a simple puppet theatre for the class might involve looking for pictures and information about puppet theatres, and asking other children about their experiences and preferences for different types of puppet theatres. If several designs are made by different children in a group, then they may decide to have a vote to find the favourite design to use. (All of these examples would involve Data Handling for a real purpose.)

As part of the planning, the children may need to make preliminary measurements to decide on sizes and/or quantities of materials required. For example, the designing of a class book might require judgements about size by comparing paper sizes available with existing, large class books. The tuck shop mentioned earlier needs decisions to be made about how much 'stock' to have. The puppet theatre would need to correspond to the heights of the children standing or kneeling behind it, or else the sizes of the puppets to be used.

FIGURE 5.9

Making decisions about the materials to be used starts the making process. In the subsequent measuring, cutting and shaping of materials, children will undoubtedly often meet problems and difficulties to solve (Using and Applying mathematics). For example, Andrew was trying to make a paper glove and drew round his hand twice to make the front and back of it to stick together. Of course it was far too small! Suggestions from the group were:

- try someone else's hand that's bigger;
- do your own hand, but make it a bit bigger all round;
- make it three-dimensional!

Several children joined in trying to make paper gloves (someone even tried making the finger tips longer). Eventually there were two successes. Andrew had painstakingly sellotaped side pieces between all the fingers to make his glove three-dimensional. Lori had simply made two enormous 'giant's' hands and stuck them together, almost as a joke, because everyone's attempts were two small. 'Look it really fits!!' she said.

I am particularly fond of designing and making at Key Stage 1 because it shifts the control and the ideas so firmly over to the child instead of the teacher. We simply have to step back and let the children do the deciding, allowing them to reject our ideas and suggestions in preference to their own or their friend's. Vivienne Doughty, in *Child Education* (February 1995), describes how children made models of a room in a house:

'The results were wonderful because we understood the planning and thought that had gone into them, even though they were not objects of beauty.'

How very important this is! Children need these opportunities in mathematics too, i.e. to make their own decisions and try out their own ideas. The mathematics involved in Design and Technology will therefore be especially valuable in helping children to behave as mathematicians. Shape, Space and Measures, in particular, are well explored in Design and Technology work. Almost any product will have involved the children in:

- experiencing and learning about the properties of both two-dimensional and three-dimensional shapes;
- comparing sizes and measuring component parts as necessary;
- creating and talking about movements between various parts, either in the finished product or in the construction of it.

Throughout the designing and making processes, some useful Shape, Space and Measures questions might be:

- What kind of shape/size will we need?
- Is it better to have too much or too little?
- Would it help to draw a plan or make a simple model of it first?
- How many of those will you need? Do they need to be the same size?
- What sort of shape might fit best onto here?
- Can you describe how you want it to move?
- What shape or size might help the movement? Try it and see. Why do you think that works/doesn't work?
- What would definitely not be the right shape or size?

Children will get better at making and monitoring decisions to solve problems and will develop their mathematical reasoning best if they are involved in evaluating the designing and making process that they went through. It is so important to build in time to discuss with children their views about their product.

INFORMATION TECHNOLOGY (IT)

Children are expected to use IT to communicate and handle information, and to support their problem solving, recording and expressive work.

For the most part, IT will be built into mathematics rather than the other way round, but there are some aspects of mathematics – Data Handling; Shape, Space and Measures and Using and Applying – that will naturally be found within much IT work. Whenever there is some information (or data) to collect, sort and classify, IT might be used to do this and to present the results afterwards using tables, charts and simple graphs. There must be a real purpose for the data that is important to the children involved, so that they can think about what the results mean. The context for the data may well not be mathematics (i.e. it could be a scientific or environmental study, for example), but the very creation and use of databases to sort information, search it or make comparisons will be teaching children to collect, record and interpret data as described in the Programme of Study for Number. (IT allows children to deal with far more data than would otherwise be possible, and to organise it in a greater variety of ways.)

Programmable toys, such as Valiant Roamer or turtle, enable children to create routes using turns and numbers to represent distances. Whatever the context for the activity, the mathematics of Shape, Space and Measures will be present and explored.

ART, CRAFT AND DESIGN

When children are experimenting with pattern, texture, colour, line, tone, shape, form and space, they will at the same time be developing their mathematical understanding of Shape, Space and Measures. They are to be given opportunities to explore and use two- and three-dimensional media, working on a variety of scales. (This includes drawing, painting, printmaking, collage and sculpture.)

If children plan their own art work, making decisions about what shapes and sizes of materials to use, then there will be a greater depth of mathematics involved. They will need to look very closely at shapes and forms around them, gather ideas and decide on a way forward. The teacher needs to take a back seat and support this process with appropriate open-ended questions. For example, some of the more mathematical questions and ideas might be:

- How could you find out what it really looks like?
- How else could you get ideas for it?
- Look very closely … what details can you see? What else?
- Try recording some ideas (e.g. sketches and notes).
- Do you know how big/small you'd like it to be?
- What materials might you use? Would it help to mix different types of materials?
- What do you need to do first? Then what?
- Are you pleased with it so far? Do you need any more ideas or materials to help solve any problems?
- I like this pattern/shape. Did you plan it or did it 'just happen'?!
- Have you thought about …? Have you seen this …?

There are likely to be many opportunities to draw children's attention to and to discuss:

- patterns:
- various properties of regular and irregular shapes (two dimensional and three dimensional);
- symmetry;
- positions;
- rotations/turns;

- sizes (length, area, mass/weight, height, thickness, perimeter, width, etc.);
- lines, points, spaces, regions.

These things will be important – and integral – to the art, craft and design work being done. A school recently decided to work together to create a huge appliquéed banner depicting an oak tree. An enormous amount of work went into its planning and execution. The children were involved in selecting materials (fabrics and threads) and stitching their various creations (e.g. leaves, bark, animals, spiders, flowers, etc.) onto the background, and had concentrated hard on their sewing, sitting 'cross-legged like tailors, completely absorbed in their own contribution'. They obviously shared in the excitement when the banner was finally finished and hung on display. Whilst admiring the final result, I couldn't help but wonder whether the teachers and helpers hadn't taken a bit too much control over the whole project; that it was the product of *their* enthusiasm we gazed at. The planning and designing stages didn't seem to have involved the children very much, beyond each class agreeing whether to do leaves, clouds or flowers, etc. Where were the children's *own* representations of oak leaves? How did they choose which child's design to use? Who drew the outline of the tree and made it the correct size? What problems did the children have to solve? Who organised the rota for which class used the sewing room when? Who did the outlines of the butterflies and animals? Who drew the outline of the green 'grass' fabric? Where were the children's plans for organising how to proceed? What were the things they tried that didn't work?

It seems as though the adults were almost *too* involved. They had very successfully organised and controlled a 'factory of young tailors' (i.e. the children in the sewing room), but hadn't quite stood back enough to see how the children themselves could also have been involved in the management and design parts of the project, where so much more opportunity for learning can occur. Opportunities for learning present themselves the more we stand back and consider whether the children themselves can do something that we are about to do. This is true for checking, marking, preparing materials, organising, planning, evaluating, designing, deciding, tidying, answering ... almost anything that requires any thought and that concerns the children's work.

CONCLUSION

STRANDS OF MATHEMATICS	Science	Geography	Music	English	History	PE	Design and Technology	Information Technology	Art, Craft and Design
Making and monitoring decisions to solve problems	X	X				X	X		X
Developing mathematical language and communication	X	X	X	X				X	
Developing mathematical reasoning	X	X		X	X	X	X	X	X
Developing an understanding of place value									
Understanding relationships between numbers and developing methods of computation			X						
Solving numerical problems	X								
Classifying, representing and interpreting data	X	X			X		X	X	
Understanding and using patterns and properties of shape	X	X		X		X	X	X	X
Understanding and using properties of position and movement	X	X		X		X	X	X	X
Understanding and using measures	X	X	X		X	X	X	X	X

Title above table: **Summary of the Mathematical Strengths of Other Subjects** — *Other Subjects*

FIGURE 5.10

There is plenty of opportunity to build Data Handling and some aspects of Shape, Space and Measures into your planning for other areas of the curriculum (or other subjects). If one activity can lead to learning in more than one subject, then we can 'economise' on curriculum time. You may need to have the confidence to omit some of the mathematics presented in your published scheme, for example, because it is better covered by your schemes of work for other subjects. This is likely to be particularly true of Data Handling. In contrast, Number work is rarely the focus of other areas of the curriculum and will need to be planned in conjunction with topics, everyday activities and your mathematics scheme of work.

It is also possible that a mathematics theme will serve other subjects. For example:

Routes   ⟶   Geography
Pattern   ⟶   Art and Design
Movement ⟶   PE
Time   ⟶   History and Music

Mathematics, as described in this chapter, will be occurring naturally within many other subjects, whether or not you draw the children's attention to it. It seems a pity to let it hide there unnoticed when we could be using it more explicitly to further develop children's mathematical understanding, at no extra cost in terms of curriculum time.

SUMMING UP SECTION A

The overview of The Hidden Mathematics Curriculum (figure 5.11) shows the types of mathematical experiences to be found within many aspects of Key Stage 1 children's school lives that are not specifically set up as mathematics. Some of these mathematical experiences will occur incidentally and spontaneously as you or the children notice something mathematical in what's happening and focus upon it with an individual, group or whole class. For example, at 'Newstime', either you or a child might suddenly notice and talk about the repeating pattern of colours in a giant pack of new felt pens, and then you might spontaneously play a game with them by hiding them behind your back and seeing if anyone can remember the sequence of colours or estimate how many pens were in the pack. The first type of spontaneous mathematics will always be part of a Key Stage 1 classroom. It is extremely important and cannot be planned for. An awareness of mathematics is all that is needed. But the second idea could be developed into a game that is used several times or even at every Newstime, and eventually could be

Overview of the Hidden Mathematics Curriculum

	Using and Applying	Number	Data Handling	Shape and Space	Measures
Chapter 3 Class 'Projects'					
Making huge models	✓		✓		
Organising real events	✓	✓	✓		
Solving real problems	✓	✓	✓		
Making displays and decorations	✓			✓	✓
Making class books	✓			✓	✓
Creating special areas	✓			✓	✓
Chapter 4 Everyday Activities					
Register time	✓	✓	✓		
Collecting money	✓	✓	✓		
Structure of the day	✓				✓
Assemblies	✓	✓			✓
Date, calendar and weather	✓	✓			✓
Birthdays	✓	✓			✓
Going out to play	✓	✓	✓		✓
News time	✓	✓			
Getting changed	✓	✓			✓
Getting into groups	✓	✓			
Lining up	✓	✓			
Library	✓	✓	✓	✓	✓
Playing/choosing	✓	✓	✓	✓	✓
Singing	✓	✓			
Cooking	✓	✓	✓		✓
Tidying up	✓	✓		✓	✓
Story time	✓	✓			✓
Home time	✓	✓		✓	✓
Chapter 5 Other Areas of the Curriculum					
Science	✓	✓	✓	✓	✓
Geography	✓		✓	✓	✓
Music	✓	✓			✓
English	✓			✓	
History	✓		✓		✓
PE	✓			✓	✓
Design and Technology	✓		✓	✓	✓
Information Technology	✓		✓	✓	✓
Art, Craft and Design	✓			✓	✓

FIGURE 5.11 *Overview of The Hidden Mathematics Curriculum*

shared with other Key Stage 1 colleagues. Some teachers are already beginning to jot down and collect together the things they each do that focus upon mathematics within everyday class activities, 'projects', play, etc. Ideas can then be shared between teachers and perhaps made into an extra-curricular mathematics document (or resource) to complement your scheme of work. It would be possible to link the ideas to relevant aspects of the Programmes of Study or to your own set of mathematics themes.

PLANNING FOR EXTRA-CURRICULAR MATHEMATICS

- Focus on one part of the school day (or event) that is not set up as mathematics, e.g. a daily routine, another area of the curriculum.
- Jot down anything you or the children do that uses mathematics, from one-off ideas to fully-fledged activities.
- Organise the sharing of these ideas amongst colleagues.
- Link the ideas to the most relevant aspect(s) of the Programme of Study (and/or to appropriate mathematics themes).
- Set a date for your next time to collect and share ideas.

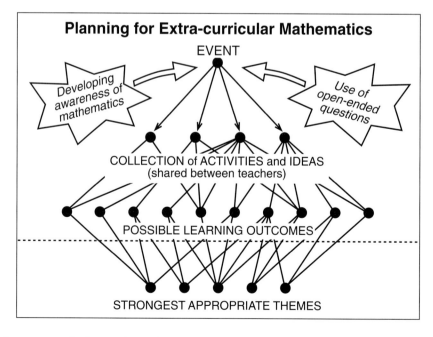

FIGURE 5.12 *Planning for extra-curricular mathematics*

In this way, some ideas can feed directly into your mathematics curriculum planning for certain times in the year when they could be given a stronger focus. For example, the ideas shared for mathematics within PE might feed directly into your planning for some work on Shape and Space, alongside a focus on some of the play activities.

The most important thing of all in using parts of the children's school day that are not set up as mathematics is to focus on what is quite naturally there, without contriving anything. Class projects, everyday activities, and other areas of the curriculum can provide natural contexts and real purposes for Using and Applying many aspects of mathematics. We should never underestimate the value of this kind of mathematics.

SECTION B

THE MATHEMATICS CURRICULUM TIME

This section includes:

CHAPTER 6
Mathematics Themes

CHAPTER 7
Creating Mathematics Activities

CHAPTER 8
Mathematical Moments

SUMMING UP SECTION B

This part of the book focuses upon those times in the school day which are planned primarily for mathematics. This may take the form of children working around a mathematics theme, using published scheme materials, engaging in mathematics that has been derived from a topic, joining in with class mathematics games and number songs, devising a mathematics trail or holding a mathematics open day. Anything, in fact, that takes mathematics consciously as its starting point.

INTRODUCTION TO SECTION B

'If children are to encounter the true nature of mathematics, they must be provided with experiences which enable them to recognise that the subject is made up of an infinity of fascinating and interrelated structures.'

Frobisher

6

MATHEMATICS THEMES

This chapter includes:
- Planning a mathematics theme
- Fun days
- Conclusion

'Some schools […] were beginning to move to an approach which was based on a sequence of longer planned units of work, each focusing on a particular maths theme. Within this theme, pupils experienced and/or explored different aspects of related mathematical ideas, addressing statements over a range of relevant levels and, in some cases, spanning attainment targets.'

(SCAA)

This is most certainly the way forward for what is planned as mathematics in the classroom. A mathematics theme allows Using and Applying to operate within a region of mathematics, which is necessary if it is to bring together different aspects of related mathematics at a variety of levels.

PLANNING A MATHEMATICS THEME

Choosing a theme

A mathematics theme is not so difficult to plan. We are quite used to planning themes and topics in Key Stage 1. The first thing, of course, is to decide upon one, making sure that the overall set of themes for each year will provide a good balance and coverage of the Programme of Study. The simplest way to do this would be to choose from the seven strands of the Programmes of Study for Number, Shape, Space and Measures. Themes taken from Data Handling, Shape and Space, and Measures are often undertaken alongside children's Number work, which continues (in a more linear fashion) all the time. But it is important that the number work itself is planned around themes, too, so that connections between related aspects of number can be made.

'The pupils whose understanding of number was most secure were those taught in classes where they encountered a variety of experiences which helped them to appreciate mathematical relationships.'

(OFSTED, 1993)

Also, in planning for each strand, you would have to think about possible connections to other areas of mathematics and indeed other areas of the curriculum. For example, a theme based upon 'Classifying, representing and interpreting data' would involve links to Measures and Shape work as well as a very strong link to science.

A way to organise mathematics themes that would each quite naturally cross boundaries within and between aspects of the Programmes of Study would be to draw up and choose from a list of rich mathematical ideas such as those in figure 6.1.

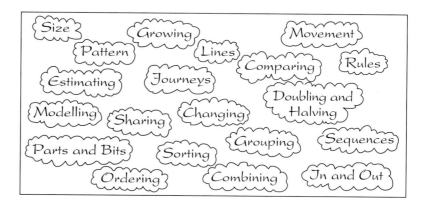

FIGURE 6.1 *Frobisher's (1992) seven operational processes of sorting, matching, comparing, sequencing, ordering, combining and changing are incorporated here.*

Size, for example, would involve sizes of Number as well as all aspects of Measure. In Data Handling, children can measure and compare sizes and amounts (e.g. is the person with the largest handspan also the tallest? How much seed do the birds eat each day?). Even in Shape work, it is good to explore different sizes of the same shape in order to determine what the properties of a certain shape really are. Number work occurs in almost every theme, with varying emphases on different aspects of it.

Whatever the theme, the Programme of Study will help to provide sub-themes that, without contrivance, are linked most closely to your title. One of the lessons learned from pre-National Curriculum Topic Work in Primary Schools was that, far too easily, every aspect of the curriculum can get squeezed into a chosen topic, sometimes by quite tenuous links. It does not matter if whole chunks of the mathematics curriculum are more or less excluded in your mathematics theme because the themes do not usually continue for more than two or three weeks, and because what is missed out can inform your choice of the next theme, ensuring a balance of coverage over the year.

Set of activities

When you have your sub-themes, you can 'brainstorm' ideas and sift through all your mathematics resources (e.g. schemes, games, puzzles, this book (!), songs and stories, videos, etc.) to build up a set of activities that are all related to your theme. (Just use bookmarks and scribbled references at this stage.) You will probably find that you have quite an odd collection of all sorts of different types of activity, from workcards to games. This is exactly what you need. The more varied the collection, the better. You might also have far too much for the time you can spend on the theme. This is good, too, for the next stage is to choose and develop the activities you are actually going to use, on the basis of certain criteria:

- Open-endedness: which activities will allow children to make some of their own choices and allow children to work at different levels?
- Manageability: which activities do I know well and have every confidence to use? Which activities don't need me too much?
- Purposes: which activities are based on a real reason to do them or real problem to solve? Or something intriguing to explore?

These are the most important criteria of all, for you need some activities that will do these things, but in the end you would ideally like to achieve a balance of activities that:

- has some choice within it for the children (e.g. 'there are four games. Choose at least one of them');
- uses a variety of practical equipment (e.g. everyday objects, mathematical materials, the indoor and outdoor environment, the children themselves, technological aids such as calculators, computers, programmable toys, etc.);
- has a range of activities, from teacher-led to those that children can perform independently of you;
- allows children to work as individuals, as pairs, in small groups and as a class;
- has some short (less than twenty minutes), some medium (about a session) and some long (several sessions);
- leads to a variety of recording (e.g. children's own methods,

Planning Checklist

THEME: PATTERNS and RULES — Activities (showing choices, if any)

Sub themes:
- Repeating patterns
- Growing/shrinking sequences
- Function machines

Category		Spot the pattern	Singing/clapping	Action/PE	Display table	Shopping game	Problem songs	Pattern day	Function box	Secret functions	Calculator functions	Colourful unknown
Open endedness	Open	●		●	●			●	○	●	●	●
	Partly open		●			●	●		●	○	○	
	Closed											
Teacher time	Teacher intensive	●	●				●	○				
	Some input required			●		●		●	○	●	○	
	Little or no input				●				●		●	●
Grouping	Individual							○	●		○	●
	Pairs			●	○		●	●	●		○	●
	Small group					●	●	●		○	●	
	Whole class	●	●					●	○			
Time	Short session	●	●			●			●			
	Full session			●	●			●	●		●	●
	Several sessions				○			○	●			
Recording	None	●	●	●					●			
	Children's own	○	○	○	○	○	●	●			●	
	Worksheet	○					●			●	●	●
	Class/group display				●			●				
Way of working	Practical	●	●	●	●		●	●	●		○	○
	Mental imagery	●		○		●	●	○	●	●	●	
	Pencil and paper							○	○	○	●	○
	Discussion	●	●	●	○	○	○	○	●			
Type of activity	Problem solving							●	●	●	●	●
	Investigational	●	○	●				●				○
	Game/puzzle	●			○	●		○	●	●	●	○
	Making/creating		●	●	●		○	●				
	Play		●	●				●				
	Experience and practice				○				○	○	○	
	Real-life	●						●				
AT1 strands	Deciding		●	●	●		●	●				●
	Communicating	●	●	●	●		●	●		●	○	○
	Reasoning	●	●	●	●	●	●	●	●	●	●	●
Assessment strengths	AT1				●	●		●	●			○
	AT2	●	●	●	●	●	●	●	●	●	●	●
	AT3			○	○			○				

○ means 'possibly'

FIGURE 6.2a *Planning checklist*

Planning Checklist		Activities (showing choices, if any)													
THEME:															
Sub themes:															
Open endedness	Open														
	Partly open														
	Closed														
Teacher time	Teacher intensive														
	Some input required														
	Little or no input														
Grouping	Individual														
	Pairs														
	Small group														
	Whole class														
Time	Short session														
	Full session														
	Several sessions														
Recording	None														
	Children's own														
	Worksheet														
	Class/display														
Way of working	Practical														
	Mental imagery														
	Pencil and paper														
	Discussion														
Type of activity	Problem solving														
	Investigational														
	Game/puzzle														
	Making/creating														
	Play														
	Experience and practice														
	Real-life														
AT1 strands	Deciding														
	Communicating														
	Reasoning														
Assessment strengths	AT1														
	AT2														
	AT3														

FIGURE 6.2b

worksheets, none at all, classbooks, displays, etc.);
- has a variety of types of activity (e.g. games, puzzles, investigations, problems to solve, play, making and creating, etc.);
- has a variety of modes of working (e.g. practical, imaginative/ mental imagery, pencil and paper, discussion, etc.)

It does not matter if your set of activities for one theme doesn't have this balance. But you need to know what's missing so that you can build it into future work, therefore creating a balance as the year progresses. The list should be used as a checklist, either informally looking through and making a mental note of what you need to develop in the future, or more formally by actually filling in the type of 'blob' chart in figure 6.2 now and again. (The blank chart is provided for this purpose.)

Operation 'Using and Applying'

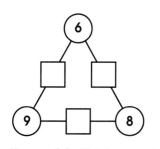

FIGURE 6.3 *'Arithmagons'*

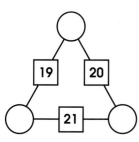

FIGURE 6.4

Before the planning checklist in figure 6.2 was used for Patterns and Rules, the activities were all considered in terms of Using and Applying. Each was studied in order to make it more open-ended, so that children could bring their own ideas into the tasks at their own level. The line in the checklist for closed activities should be as empty as possible, although there will be some activities that are quite rightly closed at some point (these are labelled as partly open). A closed, specific starting point can provide the basis of a more open investigation later (e.g. add up pairs of corner numbers to find the totals to write in the boxes (figure 6.3). Now invent some of your own for each other where the boxes are filled in but not the circles (figure 6.4)). A problem might only have one solution and therefore be closed at the end, but can be open-ended in terms of the many different ways of approaching the task (e.g. given the problem of finding what numbers go into the circles, some children may use lots of trial and error with mental arithmetic, others may use cubes and others may use logical reasoning with a calculator to check). Remember that it is still possible for very open activities to be concentrated around the exploration of a specific aspect of the Programme of Study.

Even the worksheets went through this 'push' to incorporate more Using and Applying. Some were built around a more practical activity, some were reproduced without numbers so that children could choose their own, some led to a puzzle or a problem for a partner to solve, etc. It is always worth making this extra effort for Using and Applying in your planning. Many activities, workcards or worksheets can be vastly improved by sometimes quite minor changes (see chapter 8).

Possible learning

'Objectives for learning must be flexible enough to allow the teaching to fit the direction learning takes, and not the other way about.'

(Clemson and Clemson, 1994)

If you are confident about the mathematics curriculum, you will always be aware of the potential for focusing on different aspects of mathematics in all you do, including noticing when children are being mathematical (e.g. deciding, discussing, reasoning) in their work. It will help you to develop this confidence if you look through the Programmes of Study and the Attainment Target Level Descriptions, jotting down (or highlighting on a photocopy) those aspects of mathematics that are particularly relevant to your set of activities.

Checklist for planning a mathematics theme

- Decide on a theme (looking back to what aspects of mathematics were not covered last time). Jot down the most appropriate subthemes.
- Rummage through all your mathematics resources finding relevant activities and ideas. Think of any natural links to other aspects of mathematics, other areas of the curriculum and the children's everyday lives
- Select some activities that are:
  - open-ended;
  - manageable;
  - purposeful.

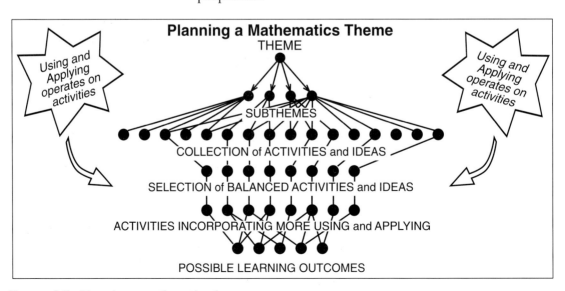

FIGURE 6.5 *Planning a mathematics theme*

Choose and adapt from the other activities and ideas to create a balanced unit of work.

- Incorporate as much Using and Applying as possible into each activity and check the balance.
- Be aware of the possible learning.

An example of a mathematics theme in action: Estimating

Here is a selection of possible activities from which to choose.

ESTIMATION BONANZA

An event to start off and finish the theme. The classroom is laid out with a selection of things to estimate, including numbers of things as well as a whole range of measures.

- Number
  - About how many petals are on this flower?
  - About how many items of clothing are in this dressing up box?
  - About how many people are on this 'Where's Wally' page?
  - About how many coins are in this tin?

- Linear Measurements
  - About how far along this strip of paper would these bead laces reach?
  - Mark your name on the playground in chalk for whereabouts you think these metre sticks would get to, laid end to end from the wall.
  - About how many cubes deep is the water in our water tray?
  - Which piece of string just fits round a PE hoop?
  - Cut a piece of wool that would just fit around our big oak tree.

- Area
  - About how many sheets of newspaper would cover the carpet area?
  - About how many sequins would cover this mermaid's tail?
  - Cut or find a piece of material that you think would just cover the computer keyboard or mouse.

- Volume
  - Which stone do you think will make the water come up to the top when it is dropped in?
  - About how many of these books will fit in the box?
  - Which model uses the most cubes?

- Capacity
  - Which container holds about the same amount as this milk bottle?
  - About how many cupfuls of counters are in here?
  - About how many of these buckets of sand are in the sand tray?

- Mass/Weight
  - About how many wooden beads would balance with our hamster?
  - Make a lump of plasticine that you think would balance with this shell.

- Time
  - About how many times could we say 'Supercalofragalistiespiallidoscious' whilst this 10-second tocker goes?
  - How many could we count to whilst the water is emptying from this bottle?
  - About how many times could we run around the playground whilst Tristan runs round the school field?

- Temperature
  - Do you think these ice cubes will melt before lunch, before afternoon playtime, before home time, after home time or sometime during school tomorrow?

- Angle
  - Which bottle top do you think can turn the most and least?

There are many ways to organise the Estimation Bonanza:

- Groups of children can be taken round the items with a classroom helper throughout the morning whilst the rest of the class works on other things.
- Pairs of children can start in different places and move round the items like a 'circus'.
- You could select some items to do together as a class, making verbal estimates and choosing different children to offer their ideas.
- Half the class can be 'stationed' in pairs at each of the items to record the estimates whilst the other half move round in pairs doing the estimating. Then they can swap over.

You need to emphasise all the time that you are not at all interested in anyone getting estimates that are exactly right, only in what everyone agrees is sensible (i.e. could have been right). The children themselves should do the counting and measuring to find the results once everyone has made their estimates. They should think about the largest range of estimates that *they* would consider sensible or possible (both above and below their results) before discussing each item as a class.

If children have recorded their estimates, it is extremely important that no one is ridiculed for estimates that are 'way out'. Young children will have to make wild guesses if they have little or no previous experience of an item in the Bonanza. Estimates must be either anonymous or else only informally kept by the estimators themselves. Whether verbally given or informally recorded, children should be encouraged to change their minds during testing if the testing is done together. Stop halfway through if possible and ask if anyone would like to change their estimate. Stop near the end and offer them the chance to adjust their estimate again. Estimates can only be improved with experience, which is gained during testing. (The Estimation Bonanza should be a learning experience, not a test.)

NOW YOU SEE IT, NOW YOU DON'T

Children work in pairs with a tray, a covering cloth and some objects. They take turns to secretly set the tray with a number of items and then uncover it very briefly so that the other person sees what's there, but doesn't have time to count. An estimate is given before they can count the items together. No recording is required. Do they get better at it? Is it easier with assorted items? Is it easier if the items are arranged neatly instead of jumbled up?

CONSECUTIVE NUMBER RESULTS

Any two or more numbers that are next to each other in the counting sequence are consecutive numbers. The result when consecutive numbers are added is given to the child, who then has to try to work out which ones they could be. For example, 9 could be the result of adding 2 + 3 + 4 (or 4 + 5). There will be a lot of estimating and trial and error involved. Calculators should be provided so that the children's thinking and estimating can be easily checked as they work. This activity works well with children in pairs (of similar ability) who devise results for each other, setting their own challenges (figure 6.6). Can every number be made by adding consecutive numbers?

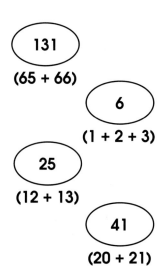

FIGURE 6.6 *Consecutive Number Challenges*

TRAFFIC LIGHTS

Use a page of calculations from a published scheme (or workcard) and a set of three coloured crayons for each child. For each calculation, they must use red first to write down an answer that they know cannot possibly be correct. Then yellow to write an answer of about the right magnitude (an estimate) or a range of possible answers (e.g. 'between ten and twenty'). Finally they should calculate the true answer and write it in green. (If you keep a bank of suitable workcards or photocopied pages for this, then children can select for themselves a set of calculations that they think will be not too easy and not too hard. Calculators will help some children to challenge themselves further, without detracting from the estimating involved.)

CUPS OF WATER AT PLAYTIME

You need some plastic cups and some clean bottles, jugs or buckets. In pairs (or threes), children should estimate about how many cups of water they will need to serve to their class outside at playtime (some children might not want any and others might drink two or three cupfuls). They should then keep a record of the number of cupfuls served. Halfway through playtime, they should be allowed to change their first estimate if they want to, and again near the end. (They would then finish the activity with a first, second and third estimate as well as the final count.) If two or three children do this at each playtime and lunchtime over several days, it becomes possible for most children to have a go.

- Are the results the same for each playtime?
- Is it the same everyday? Why? Why not?
- What about if orange squash is used instead?
- Try estimating how much water or squash will be needed as well as how many cupfuls served.
- Is it better to under-estimate or over-estimate in this activity?

CLASSROOM SEARCH

1   Children work either individually or in pairs and choose an item in the classroom to draw, estimate how many there are and/or estimate something about its size (e.g. length, thickness, etc.) in suitable non-standard or standard units. They then proceed to count and measure, with the freedom to make revised estimates during the testing. Possible items are shown in figure 6.7. You may like to provide a recording sheet, like the one in figure 6.8. The children should be encouraged to be as inventive as they like in choosing items to count and measure (e.g. cracks in the wall, dead leaves on a plant, zip teeth, etc.). You may like to include the outdoor environment too.

2   Children choose a number (e.g. 12) and/or a measure (e.g. six handspans, half a metre, ten conkers) and look around the classroom for as many examples of it that are about right, recording their findings. For example, the number 12 might

lead to drawings such as those in figure 6.9. (The number in brackets represents the actual number.)

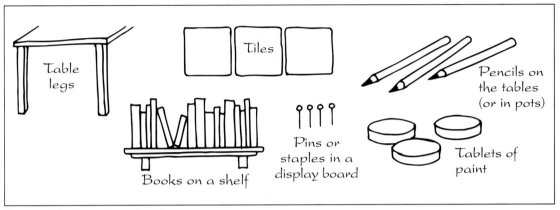

FIGURE 6.7 *Items for estimation*

Object	About how many?	How many?

Object	What to measure?	What units?	Estimate	Measure

FIGURE 6.8 *Recording sheets for estimation*

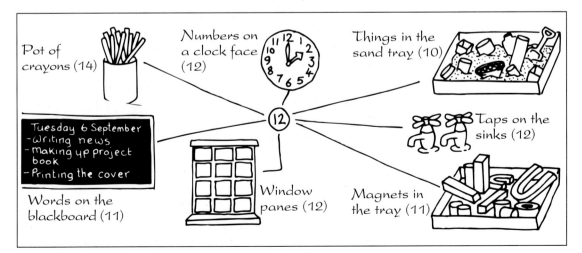

FIGURE 6.9 *Discovering 'about twelve' in the classroom*

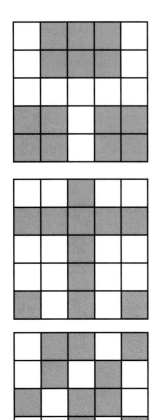

FIGURE 6.10 *Square Patterns*

These classroom search activities work best when a small group of children is involved (perhaps in pairs), with as much choice as possible for objects and measures. However, you can easily adapt them to focus on a particular measure or measuring instrument.

SQUARE PATTERNS

A large group of children each need to choose their own secret number between 5 and 20 (having first of all estimated and counted how many squares there are in the five-by-five grids (figure 6.10)). Then everyone colours their own number of squares in a pattern or randomly (they must decide what suits their number, imagining it before starting) on their own twenty-five square. As children are finishing, you can stop the group from time to time to look at and estimate some of the secret numbers:

'How many do you think Sébastien has?'
'Is that estimate quite close to your secret number, Sébastien?'
'Is it *about* that number?'

Try comparing three twenty-five squares, putting them in order from most to least squares coloured without counting (just by estimating). Get the three children to run off out of earshot and verify the order by telling each other their numbers ('My number was 19, what was yours? So mine did have the most, and they were right about your two.' 'Yes! You were right this time!').

Try looking for any two twenty-five squares (everyone puts them down in front of them) that the children think might have about the same number coloured. Count them and see. Try to find some more examples of the same number. How different do they look? Either as a group or afterwards in pairs, challenge the children to put all the twenty-five squares in order from most to least squares coloured.

PLAY 'PIN THE TAIL ON THE DONKEY'

To do this, children need to estimate whereabouts (i.e. how far in from the side, how far up from the bottom) the tail should go, imagining the distances involved and feeling the edges of the board. Let them have several goes each, so that they can experience getting better at it.

ABOUT HALF

Set up some objects and ideas that children can estimate and then measure and calculate half of:

- Whereabouts is half way through this book?
- Where is your 'half' height?
- Where is half way across the classroom?
- Where is half way up this bowl?
- When were you half as old as you are now?
- Get about half of these straws out of the box.
- Where is half way across this page?
- About how many circles or bubbles can you draw in half a minute?
- Find half the mass/weight of this plasticine …

This activity could form the basis of a 'fun day' about halves (see page 12).

- Try the same activity for 'twice as many' and 'twice as big (long, wide, heavy, etc.)', with the children estimating and calculating or measuring a variety of objects, recording in their own way.
- Try the same activity for 'about the same as'.
- Try it for estimating 'about the centre of' various shapes. Finding the actual centre can be quite a challenge and can be offered as a problem-solving activity after estimating.

DESIGN AND TECHNOLOGY

Plan for the children to design and make something during your mathematics theme work on estimating (thereby creating value-added learning). Apart from emphasising the estimation required naturally by such tasks, it is also good to ask children to consider whether it is better to overestimate or underestimate the numbers of items, sizes of materials and time required, etc. For example, in wallpapering a dolls' house room, it is better to slightly overestimate the amount of paper required and trim it to fit. But in mixing powder paints it is better to underestimate the amount of water required and then add slightly more until the correct consistency is reached.

FIGURE 6.11

HIDDEN MATHEMATICS CURRICULUM

There will be many occasions in children's everyday school lives that either naturally require estimating or could easily do so. (See section A for possibilities.)

CONCLUSION/POSSIBLE LEARNING

The main mathematical focus of this theme on estimating is number work and measures. It would make sense to plan a theme on Shape and Space or Data Handling to follow it, or a stronger focus on number (e.g. addition and subtraction facts). Possible learning includes:

- ability to represent work with objects, pictures, symbols or simple diagrams and discuss it;
- ability to organise work and check results;
- ability to explain thinking;
- ability to count;
- ability to read and write numbers;
- development of mental calculation strategies;
- mental recall of some number facts;
- measurement and ordering of objects using direct comparison;
- ability to choose and use everyday non-standard and standard units to measure length, capacity, mass and time, in a range of contexts;
- gaining a feeling for the appropriate size of an answer.

'To continue to work in a thematic way does require a lot of planning, as well as an ability to identify aspects of the curriculum as they emerge from the children's work. This is treating the National Curriculum truly as a curriculum rather than as a syllabus, and watching to identify its presence in the learning outcomes of the children's work.'

(Leone Burton, 1994)

Important features of mathematics themes

- Activities can often be done in any order.
- Activities are mostly open-ended enough to allow children to work at different levels.
- The mathematics can span several areas of the Programmes of Study.
- A balanced set of themes for the year will create your scheme of work.
- Existing published scheme material becomes a resource to feed into the themes.

FUN DAYS

Your planning for a mathematics theme can often include a 'fun day'. Fun days are a way to focus upon one tiny aspect of mathematics (e.g. the number 8, halves, cubes) and to build it into as many different contexts as possible, all within one day. Children will be able to understand a mathematical concept far more easily if a whole range of examples of the concept are experienced and discussed within a very short time. They will learn to separate the abstract mathematical idea from all the equipment and activities that surround it (i.e. they achieve 'disembedded' thinking, as described by Margaret Donaldson). Even in something as simple as a day of three (described below), children learn far more than the ability to estimate, count, read and write the number 3. They will learn, for example, that numbers are not only to do with counting objects; that a number of objects is not altered by changing their size, shape and position; that a number has a place in a counting sequence (the idea of ordinality); and so on.

Fun days should ultimately be planned with the children, taking a few moments from time to time to write down their ideas and suggestions for activities. The mathematical thinking and imagining that goes into this planning and sharing of ideas is as important as the day itself:

'We're going to have a Day of Three next week, when everything we can think of will be connected to three in some way. Perhaps we could have:

- Three stories about threes (e.g. 'The Three Little Pigs', 'The Three Bears', 'Snow White and the Three Dwarfs!' (we'll make that one up!)). Can you think of some other possibilities?
- A printing table for printing in three colours, with three three-sided shapes, on triangular shaped paper.
- A calculator table where 3 is the answer and you have to find as many ways as possible to end up with 3, perhaps using three numbers...
- Singing Time: three number songs where we do something funny/different on the third verse, or the verse with a 3 in it (e.g. whisper it, stand up for it).
- PE in threes, balancing on three points, using three pieces of apparatus, creating sequences of three movements.
- Everyone coming to school with three colours in their clothes.
- People bringing their packed lunch in threes (e.g. three small sandwiches, three pieces of orange, triangular-shaped cheeses).

- Three children could collect examples of threes from around the classroom to put on this tray/display.
- We could try making some plasticine threes that balance with three conkers or three shells or three pencils.
- We could choose just three toys to have in the sandpit or just three containers in the water play.

What else could we do? How shall we choose which things to do? What do we do normally that we could change to include threes?' The first time that such a day is attempted, there will probably be more input of ideas from the teacher than the children. But once the children get the idea of putting something into so many contexts and activities, they will quickly outstrip the teacher with their imaginations. Sometimes their ideas may need some negotiation/adapting in order to make them possible! (For example, Benjamin wanted to paint the classroom floor tiles in three colours. This was eventually adapted to painting huge pieces of paper divided into squares, with three children doing different designs in three colours.) Figure 6.12 gives you some possible fun-day starters.

Fun days can help young children to build mathematics concepts, to be creative, and to use and apply mathematics. After planning a fun day with the children, the day itself often works best if the children are allowed to choose the activities they wish to try, within certain agreed rules, such as 'no more than three children per activity' or ' leave it tidy and ready for someone else to have a go'. Activities can often be adapted to suit many levels of ability. For example, a 'machine' to halve numbers may be made using counters/ cubes, calculators, number lines, or simply using one-to-one matching.

Fun days can be excellent for teacher assessments. The children become involved in what they've chosen to do, and the teacher can be an observer, asking questions, listening, watching, making notes. Some teachers' comments after trying out fun days:

'It was a good starter day for our new maths theme.'

'I was worried that too many children were wandering around at first, but they soon settled and then became amazingly concentrated and involved.'

'The first one we did was not as exciting as the second one. I think it was because the children were so involved in the planning second time round and had invented so many activities themselves.'

'It was excellent for discoveries and excitement in maths, particularly for certain children.'

DAY OF STRAIGHT LINES

- Put desks/chairs in straight lines.
- Find something stripy to wear.
- Use rulers to do straight line pictures/patterns/printing.
- Walk in straight lines.
- Write with straight letters and numbers.
- Play noughts and crosses or Connect 4.
- Have sandwiches cut into strips.
- Do spagetti pictures.
- Find shapes with 3,4,5 ... straight sides.
- Do curved stitching.

Ask the children for their ideas too

DAY OF OPPOSITES

DAY OF OPPOSITES

- Start with a story if you normally end with one.
- Sit opposite someone.
- Make a model, make its opposite.
- Teacher sits on carpet, a child on teacher's chair.
- Do the opposite (e.g. 'Make more noise' means 'quieten down', 'slow down' means 'hurry up').
- Collect opposites to put opposite each other in a book or on a poster.

DAYS OF **BIG** AND SMALL

Have several small playtimes...

Small Day:
- Have miniature sand and water play (with tiny containers and pen tops).
- Do tiny writing/tiny pictures.
- Whisper the register.
- Find minibooks or short stories.
- Read about The Minpins, Lilliput...
- Bring lunch in very small pieces.
- Wear something a bit too small.
- Everyone bring the tiniest box they can find...

For BIG Day, do opposites of these things! Try bringing your packed lunch in a suitcase...

Squash everyone into the smallest space...

DAY OF SQUARES

- Draw squares in chalk on the playground that you think the whole class can stand inside, stand around, lie down in....
- Draw/paint square pictures.
- Invent a square game.
- Bring square sandwiches.
- Do square sums e.g.

$$\begin{array}{c|c} 2 & 2 \\ \hline 0 & 2 \end{array} \quad 6$$

Don't forget to ask the children for their ideas.

DAY OF HALVES

- Have half a day instead.
- Make half quantities in a recipe.
- Make half a book about halves.
- Play with only half the bricks.
- Cut shapes in half in different ways.
- Play in half the playground.
- Have two playtimes that last only half the time each.
- Collect examples of halves.
- Make a 'machine' to halve numbers.
- Find out when you're half way to your next birthday.

Other Ideas:-

Day of Symmetry
Day of Symmetry

Day of Sorting

A Pattern Day

Day of Pairs

A No Numbers Day e.g. Numbers not allowed. Cover them all up. Don't even say a number. What's difficult without them? So what do we need numbers for?

A Favourite Number Day Everyone works on their specially chosen number. Children guess each other's favourite number...

A Backwards Day

A Colour Day e.g. Day of Red

FIGURE 6.12 *Possible 'Fun Day' starters*

'Some children did several of the activities and others only did one or two, but everyone was concentrated and involved.'

'They loved being able to choose which activities to do.'

'They listened to each other much more attentively than usual when we were discussing what different people had been doing.'

'We stopped several times throughout the day to share ideas (and to reinforce the rules). Every activity seemed to get better and better as they learned about the variety of ways other children were responding.'

'Many other areas of the curriculum ended up being involved. It wasn't just maths all day.'

OTHER MATHEMATICAL EVENTS

Organising special events from time to time can bring mathematics to life for children, teachers and parents, especially if the children themselves are involved directly in the planning of them.

Assemblies

Many mathematical themes will lend themselves well to active assemblies (e.g. pattern, time) with possibilities for music, singing, art and craft, etc. (Ask the children for their ideas.) It would even be possible to do an interesting assembly on 'sums', with a wide variety of interpretations of them. For example:

- songs which calculate ('ten green bottles ... and if three green bottles should accidentally fall'... see page 72);
- tricks such as 'Choose a number; add one; add three; subtract your number; add two; subtract one' (everyone's answer is five!);
- children's dartboard with the scoring happening mentally and aloud;
- a scenario of shopping and giving change: making a mistake; checking; going back to the shop; explaining; apologising;
- games (e.g. the Differences Game, see page 136).
- puzzles to act out, e.g. 'As I was going to St Ives, ...'

Assemblies can celebrate mathematics and help children to appreciate its fascination and fun. Don't give badges for 'good efforts' in assemblies, trying to encourage children to work harder at mathematics. Let them experience the intrigue and interest within the subject for themselves. This will be far more encouraging and empowering.

Competitions and Fairs

An occasional competition or mini-mathematics fair can create a lot of enthusiasm, adding extra purpose to mathematical activities. For example:

FIGURE 6.13 *Creating a large poster based on one number*

DESIGN A NUMBER POSTER

Children work in pairs to create a large poster all based on one number (of their choosing). They should have scrap paper available to jot down and try out ideas first, and then access to a variety of crayons, paints, collage bits and pieces, etc. so that they can create as many colourful and textured ways to represent their number as possible. Judging could be by voting (see page 36), and the finished posters will make a wonderful display.

ESTIMATION SUPERSTARS

This is the same as the Estimation Bonanza on page 113, except that children record their estimates and put them centrally whilst they share out the counting, checking and/or measuring of each item. Each pair of children then needs to decide upon a range of estimates that they think should score top marks (and perhaps further ranges that could score half-marks). For example, in counting twenty-seven items of clothing in the dressing-up box, they might decide that estimates between twenty and thirty will score ten points. It is important that they allow for over-estimates as well as underestimates, and the fact that it is a competition helps children to focus upon whether the ranges are fair. In the example above, someone might argue:

'But I put thirty-one and that's only four away and Tom put twenty and that's seven away. He gets ten points and I don't!'

It is always best to let the children themselves discover these problems instead of avoiding them by telling them to do it all in a certain way. A large amount of number work and understanding about the number system can arise through this process of designing the scoring system and finding total scores. It is a full activity in itself.

OTHER IDEAS FOR COMPETITIONS

- Who can fit the most objects into a matchbox (or film-pot)? Every object must be different.

- With a piece of paper and a calculator, who can find the most ways to make twelve?
- Whose stone is the heaviest? Whose stone causes the most water to overflow from this full container?

Mathematics trails

Trails can be set up outside in the school grounds, around the school building or using the classroom only. They can be based upon specific mathematics themes and are especially good when the children themselves set them up for each other.

FOLLOWING INSTRUCTIONS

Using a number of paces (ten paces forwards, turn left …) children soon learn that different children have different sized paces and that they don't always end up in the correct place. (To solve this problem they often try to match their paces beforehand, or else write in checks along the way, such as 'You should be by the wall now'. Their discussion is almost inevitably based upon distances and measures.) When children decide to use features of the route in their instructions (e.g. 'Go to the edge of the field' or 'Face the corner by the oak tree') they often find that they need to refine their mathematical language several times before their trail works. (You will need to organise some children to be ready as 'trail-testers'.)

FOLLOWING A MAP

Children can decide how to do the maps (e.g. like plans or as picture maps) and what features will be important to mark. The route is to be marked on the map for other people to follow. If it isn't clear enough, then people will get lost and have to return to clarify and improve it. Whether following instructions and/or a map, the route will have a finishing point as the focus (perhaps to collect something or find a secret 'buried' treasure) or several stopping places at which to answer mathematical questions.

ANSWERING QUESTIONS IN DIFFERENT AREAS

For example, in the Hall:

- Where can you see a number five?
- Draw the pattern of black and white piano keys.
- What shape is the roof window?

Children can record their observations and answers in their own way, using just pictures if desired. Working in small groups or pairs can help with reading and writing problems. Some questions can be specific and others more open with several possible responses to discuss later.

A SERIES OF CLUES (LIKE A TREASURE HUNT)

The idea is to give children the first clue only (e.g. library) where they must go and hunt for the next clue. When they find it, it will tell them where to go next (e.g. door). But they might not know which door and have to hunt at several possibilities and so on.

Eventually, they will arrive at the treasure (e.g. a few small biscuits wrapped in foil) or other end point. There is an enormous amount of mathematical thinking involved in children setting up clues like this because they have to hide a clue in a place that doesn't match what's on it, and imagine the people following the clues in order to achieve the correct sequence. Children could try this if necessary using up to six classroom-based clues (e.g. cupboard, blackboard, bookshelf, etc.) first.

ARROWS, SIGNS AND SYMBOLS

The children can invent symbols using easily accessible outdoor materials (e.g. twigs, stones, daisies, leaves, seeds, etc.) and explain them so that other people can follow the route. Combinations of symbols such as those in figure 6.14 can give direction and distances. They should, of course, test out their trail and ensure that none of it can easily be disturbed by the wind or playtime, etc.

FIGURE 6.14 *A stick with a leaf to say walk ahead this way. Stones to say how many paces*

A COLLECTING TRAIL

Ask children to collect ten leaves of different shapes and sizes or choose what to collect for each number up to ten (e.g. nine daisies, eight twigs, seven stones, six blades of grass, etc.) or collect five things longer than their pencil and five things shorter than it.

Collecting trails can be used for almost any aspect of mathematics and simply involve hunting for specific examples of an idea or concept. For example, when I tried this with one of my classes, I didn't know if it was going to be at all possible, but I stood the group in front of an ordinary hedge while we were walking round looking for circles and simply asked them to look very hard for any examples of them. After a few moments, we had the ends of broken twig, tiny ladybird's spots, the centre of a flower, a spider's web (almost), the shell of an old acorn … It is amazing what can be found if you really look and give it time!

You may need to do the first one of any of these types of trails so that the children understand what to do, but there will be even more mathematical thinking involved when they create and test their own trails for each other.

Games libraries

Young children usually enjoy taking a mathematics game or puzzle home from time to time to share with their family. If the games are organised under mathematics theme headings (and labelled as such, so that parents can more easily see the mathematical purpose of the game), it will be easy to draw out particular ones that suit your theme to use in class time too.

The children, their families and you (together with any other colleagues) can slowly build up a selection of board games, card games, verbal/mental games, outdoor games, journey games (car, bus, train, walking, etc.), domino games, puzzles. If any games are not popular, try to find out why. Challenge the children to adapt and change the rules to make them more fun, writing new rules on cards to go with them. You can do this anyway to games, offering alternative versions. For example, in one class we had a large new box of commercial games boards with sheets of rules to paste on to the back of each one. I hid the sheets of rules and gave the boards to the children to invent their own games. After trialling and testing their wonderfully imaginative versions, we printed their rules using the computer and pasted them on the backs of the boards instead.

Sometimes it's useful to include a comment sheet (either per child or per game), so that parents can make suggestions and give their ideas for adapting a game.

A mathematics week

Mathematics itself can be a theme for a week. If planned well in advance it can provide the focus for a wide range of new initiatives in mathematics for your class or for the whole school. Possibilities include:

AN OPEN DAY

Invite parents, governors, pre school leaders, grandparents, any available KS2 or KS3 colleagues, etc. Involve some children in the real problem-solving of providing refreshments for the visitors. Plan to use mathematics within other areas of the curriculum (e.g. have a printing workshop for numbers and shapes, work on routes for geography, time-lines for history, etc.). Make room for any visitors to try out activities alongside the children instead of simply watching.

FOCUS ON EQUIPMENT

Make an effort to get parents and children to gather interesting-shaped boxes, lollipop sticks, used matchsticks, stones, shells, conkers, pen tops, yoghurt pots, cheese boxes, film pots, flower pots, oddments of material, buttons, cotton reels … any everyday objects that are useful for mathematics. In this way, you can replenish your stock of equipment all in one go.

At the same time, look at and evaluate your mathematics equipment as a staff, sharing ideas about its use and reordering as necessary.

WORKING FOR EACH OTHER

Challenge every class to do something for another class's benefit. For example, make them some number puzzles, invite them to a picnic in the school grounds or prepare some domino biscuits to play with them and eat.

AN ESTIMATING HALL

Set up a mini-Estimation Superstars event in the hall. Throughout the week, everyone estimates and writes down their ideas (including visitors). The winners can be announced on the last afternoon.

THE GAMES LIBRARY

This could be inaugurated during the mathematics week, providing a focus for visitors and helping as many parents as possible to know of its existence.

DISPLAY BOARDS

Every class could take responsibility for a mathematics display board in the hall and corridors, making them as active as possible (i.e. with things to try).

THE PAINTING OF THE PLAYGROUND

Having designed it and planned it beforehand (see page 49), organise teams of helpers and children to do the painting.

A TUCK SHOP

Set up a tuck shop for playtimes, selling small amounts of healthy food at low prices (e.g. small bags of grapes, boxes of raisins, cherries, lumps of cheese, etc.). Get children to find out what people like first and work out costs.

A PARENTS' EVENING

Hold a parents' evening for mathematics with an invited speaker. But make it active, so that the parents get involved in doing games, puzzles, investigations and problems for themselves. They should experience the fascination of mathematics and say things like, 'I wish it had been like this when I was at school!'

OTHER IDEAS

An assembly, a fun-day, a competition (with voting), a mathematics trail ... and any other ideas.

Of course, you wouldn't have to do all of this in a mathematics week, but the ideas are offered for you to select from and adapt to suit your circumstances. Don't be afraid to add something rather big and memorable, such as finding out how big the circle would be if everyone in the school held hands, and really try it out!

It doesn't do any harm to invite or inform the local press, so that all your efforts and the children's are appreciated on a wider scale.

Although requiring a lot of planning, these types of events can bring rich rewards in terms of the children's understanding and enjoyment of mathematics. An occasional event can be memorable and motivating for a long time afterwards.

7

CREATING MATHEMATICS ACTIVITIES

'Clearly there is a challenge facing us. We have on our side, however, a strength which is often underestimated: the immense capacity of young children to grasp difficult ideas if they are presented in ways which interest them and make sense to them.'

(Martin Hughes, 1986)

There are not many resources currently available that can, on their own, present mathematics to Key Stage 1 children in purposeful and meaningful contexts. We have to mix and match ideas into our own schemes of work. Activities often need to be adapted or invented in order to capture and sustain the children's interest, and to provide the right challenge to further their mathematical thinking. This chapter focuses on developing mathematical activities to feed into your scheme of work.

NO PAGES OF SUMS

We are about to dispense with traditional, formal pages of sums for good. There is simply no need to practise purposeless calculations out of context when there are so many better alternatives that will provide the necessary practise and much more besides. Martin Hughes emphasises the use of games to replace sums (*Children and Number*, page 181) and mentions the children themselves playing a leading role in designing and making them.

An example of a game, which helps children to practise their mental arithmetic, is 'Around the track', where children choose their own numbers to put on their own tracks (the only stipulation being that they know they can cope with them) (figure 7.1). The idea is to decide whether you need to add or subtract (and by about how many) to get to the next number on the track. The calculator checks your mental arithmetic. (If you add/subtract too much or too little, you will be closer to your target and can simply

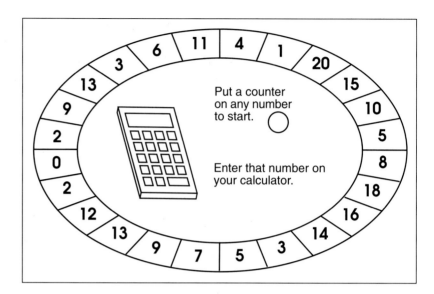

FIGURE 7.1 'Around the Track' game

do a little more. This just slows you up a bit.) You move your counter onto the next number only when the calculator displays that number, and try to go around the track as fast as you can. This activity can be adapted for all the children. At its simplest, children could simply match their numbers on the track to a calculator digit each time, using the cancel/clear button in between. Addition and subtraction can be in ones and twos, right up to hundreds and thousands. (Children in Key Stage 2 often enjoy this with multiplication and division too, or with decimals and fractions.)

Other ideas:

- Race against someone else, on the same track in opposite directions or on separate tracks.
- Time yourself. Beat your best time.
- Use cubes to help you to calculate.
- Go round the other way. Does it make any difference?
- Invent short cuts and other rules.

If they do find it too easy or too hard, then it is up to them to draw a new track that will be more fun. But children usually do get it right. They don't want to do something that is boring and too easy for them, and they don't want to make it all too difficult either (especially young children who haven't yet learned to be frightened of learning). In fact, the outcomes of open activities like this can be excellent for assessing children's level of confident understanding. (Children are only lazy if they are uninterested in the task, and they usually respond very well to being able to make their own track, the idea of racing round as fast as they can, and using a calculator.)

Throughout this chapter, I will use examples of types of activities that can replace traditional sums, so that, taken together, they will form a theme on calculation (based roughly on Year 2). It will not be exhaustive of all the many possibilities, but it should show the range of mathematics that can render formal pages of sums obsolete.

"The complete absence of sums in the early years is the only real alternative to concentrating on them. There is no viable "middle way".
(John Threlfall, 1992)

To refer back to the planning of mathematics themes (see pages 106–13), a traditional page of sums could not get through the planning process. Even if it was selected on the basis of manageability or practice, it would undergo some considerable changes when Using and Applying operated on it, for the contexts of Using and Applying are described as:

- practical tasks;
- real-life problems;
- investigating within mathematics itself.

We would have to find ways to make the sums more practical (e.g. by representing each one with a variety of equipment), generate the same sorts of sums from some real-life context (e.g. shopping) or else find ways to make them more open-ended, exploratory or investigative (e.g. decide on a total for all sums and change the first number to make them work). If, however, the emphasis on a page of sums is for the children to do them in their own way, mentally if they can, and to record how they did each one in their own way too, then the activity does become more investigative, in that children will have to decide *how* to calculate and then share each other's methods for particular sums.

The National Curriculum Programme of Study supports 'no pages of sums' and emphasises children developing their own methods of calculating, using informal ways of recording which relate to their mental work.

'… excessive practice of traditional pencil-and-paper methods out of context will act in an inhibiting way to the overall aim of raising standards in mathematics.'
(Non-Statutory Guidance E4, 1989)

The CAN curriculum (see page 25) has also provided a model of how calculating can be developed in Key Stage 1 without pages of sums.

USE OF EQUIPMENT

In Key Stage 1, children need an enormous amount of practical mathematics. Pictures of objects will never be able to replace the handling and moving around of the objects themselves. Making a display, for example, of all the different ways that children can find to represent number facts to eight, say, will involve putting together various choices of materials (figure 7.2).

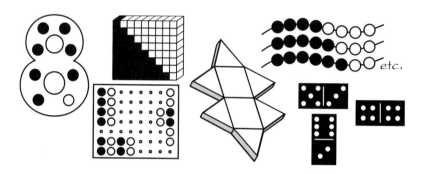

FIGURE 7.2 *Number facts display*

FIGURE 7.3

In doing so, they have to make decisions about which way round?, how spread out?, does it matter?, have we got them all represented?, etc. (Far more mathematical thinking than doing number facts to eight in their workbooks, and it helps to build the mental imagery necessary for calculation.)

Mathematical equipment can be particularly helpful for calculation if it is used well. Children should always be allowed to play freely with it before any task/activity is imposed.

'Sam (age five) adores playing in the maths corner. He often creates fascinating, huge, symmetrical patterns out of the equipment there.'

'I just couldn't get them to concentrate on the task until they'd made all their dogs and dinosaurs with the new cubes.'

In general, the children need to be in control of how the equipment is used so that it becomes a useful tool for their thinking instead of an imposed procedure to follow. This happens best when the activities have a purpose or reason, like using Base 10 material to invent games.

For example, a boy of six invented a highly successful game using the 100-square as a board and the unit-cubes as pieces to build up to fifty from opposite ends. Every time the dice was thrown, the player could choose whether to use the score himself to build up his own side or to use it to take that many units off his opponent's side, depending on how the game was going! The adding and subtracting within the game was practical and often commented on, e.g. 'If I get a five or six, I'll be in the forties ...' 'I think I'd better get you back into the thirties!' (It was teacher input that led to the naming of the rows as tens, twenties, thirties, etc. after discussing the game.)

If any mathematical equipment is underused (e.g. cuisenaire rods are sometimes found at the backs of cupboards), get it out and offer it to the children to play with and to invent games with, whilst you gather any ideas for using it from colleagues and resource books. Simply tipping cuisenaire rods out onto the table and asking children to try to work out what number each colour represents is a good starting point. The greater the variety of equipment and types of activity, the better. Dominoes and playing cards are particularly good for calculation practice.

FIGURE 7.4 *Domino Squares*

DOMINO SQUARES

- Put four dominoes into a square shape.
- Try to find four that can be arranged so that the total number of spots on each side of the square is the same (e.g. nine each side) (figure 7.4).
- Explore other ways to make your number and try doing them for other numbers.
- Which numbers are impossible/possible?

DOMINO SIXES

- Try placing all the dominoes in a line so that adjacent spots always total 6 (figure 7.5).

FIGURE 7.5 *Domino Sixes*

PAIRS

- Play 'pairs' with playing cards so that a pair is any two cards that total 10 or 9 or 8 or 7 (the children to decide on the total) (figure 7.6).

MAKE ELEVEN

Shuffle a pack of cards and start placing them (off the top of the pile) into a three-by-three array. As soon as any two cards appear

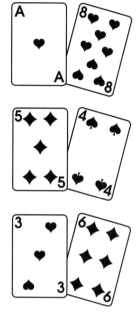

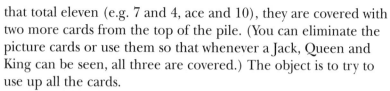

that total eleven (e.g. 7 and 4, ace and 10), they are covered with two more cards from the top of the pile. (You can eliminate the picture cards or use them so that whenever a Jack, Queen and King can be seen, all three are covered.) The object is to try to use up all the cards.

There is no one best way or one best piece of equipment to use to help children with calculating, or any other aspect of mathematics. The key features of the successful use of mathematics equipment, are:

- variety;
- discussion;
- choice;
- purpose.

FIGURE 7.6 *Pairs*

But practical work for young children does not necessarily require 'mathematical equipment'. There is an enormous amount of mathematics that can be done using:

- the children themselves (see Finger Facts, Differences Game, Jumping on an Imagined Number Track);
- everyday materials (e.g. boxes, buttons, pencils) (see PE Equipment, Hunt for Twos, Shoe Box Shopping, Crayons);
- natural objects (e.g. leaves, shells, stones) (see How Many Petals, Collecting);
- outdoor and indoor school environment (e.g. the school building, grounds, classroom furniture) (see Hymnbooks, Lunchtime Tables);
- home and local environment (see Sleeptime, Climbing Stairs, How Many Legs).

FINGER FACTS

How many different ways can you show eight with your fingers? Record them in pictures and/or symbols.

DIFFERENCES GAME

Children in pairs, hiding their hands behind their backs, each choose a number of fingers to show after saying, '1, 2, 3, Go!' at the same time. Whoever's turn it is can write down the difference as their score, e.g. I showed three and you showed seven. It's your turn, so you score four. The children can add up their scores at the end.

FIGURE 7.7

JUMPING ON AN IMAGINED NUMBER TRACK

Children stand up and imagine that they are on a big number track. They secretly choose a number to start on and actually do three jumps, then say which number they have landed on. The children can try to work out each other's starting numbers.

SHOE BOX SHOPPING

In a small group, each child has a shoe box and some small change (real money). Everyone chooses about six things to put in their shoe box for sale (e.g. rubber, book, hairclip, little bear ...). The children buy and sell from all the shoe boxes.

HUNT FOR TWOS

What can you see in the classroom that is arranged in twos? For example, tables, shoes, egg boxes. Record some examples and find the totals.

CRAYONS

How many of each colour crayon do we have? How many of each colour shall we order so that we've got the maximum number of everything?

PE EQUIPMENT

Can you share out this PE equipment amongst four groups ready for this afternoon?

HOW MANY PETALS?

How many petals are on a daisy? How many are on this daisy chain?

COLLECTING

Go outside and collect one of something, two of something else, three of something else, and so on (e.g. leaves, blades of grass, tiny stones ...). About how many things are in your collection?

HYMNBOOKS

Hymnbooks are to share one between two. How many will we need for our class, for the Key Stage 1 classes ...?

LUNCHTIME TABLES

How many children can sit at each table at lunchtime? How many tables do we need to put out today?

SLEEPTIME

What time do you go to bed? What time do you wake up? How much sleep do you have? How much of your life have you been asleep?

CLIMBING STAIRS

About how many times to you climb your stairs every day? How many stairs are there? How many stairs have you climbed this week/year/in your life?

HOW MANY LEGS

How many legs live in your house? How many fingers, etc? How many people and pets?

Activities that are based on the children's own surroundings help them to see mathematics all around them (and not just in the 'maths corner' of the classroom or in their books).

USE OF BOOKS AND WORKCARDS

'Books can never replace practical experience. However many number books your child looks at, she won't learn much unless she also counts real things for real reasons.'

(Fran Mosley, 1989)

It is an enormous challenge to find ways of writing pupil workbooks, cards, etc. for young children that will lead to the practical and purposeful activities that they need. It *can* be done, for example, by giving instructions to get pieces of equipment or by involving children's everyday lives (many experiences can be safely assumed to be common to all children: playtimes, pots of crayons, preparing a table for art work, etc.). But there are not many pupil materials like this available yet. A more natural use of pupil books/cards would be for the more abstract Using and Applying or investigating within mathematics itself. Books of starting points for exploration within number, for example, could offer activities for calculating such as the following.

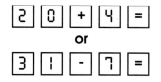

FIGURE 7.8a *Making Twenty-four*

MAKING TWENTY-FOUR

How many ways can you display twenty-four on your calculator by pressing just five keys? (Figure 7.8a) A worksheet could have several sets of five boxes for recording.

WHAT'S HAPPENING?

Choose any number to put in the first box (figure 7.8b). Work it through to the end. Try with many different numbers. What's happening? Why? Is it possible to choose a number where it won't happen? Try inventing your own line of boxes to have the same

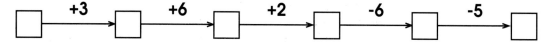

FIGURE 7.8b *What's Happening?*

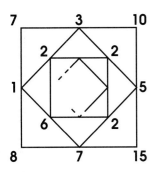

FIGURE 7.9 *Shrinking Squares*

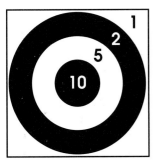

FIGURE 7.10a *Targets*

FIGURE 7.10b *Special Numbers*

effect. (A worksheet could have several linked boxes ready for the child to invent their own series.)

SHRINKING SQUARES

Draw a very large square and choose any numbers to put on the corners. Mark the midpoints of each side and write the difference between the two numbers for each side.

Join the midpoints to make the next square and keep going (figure 7.9). Find out what happens and explore: other starting numbers, putting the numbers in a different order, other shapes, how many squares it takes, etc.

TARGETS

Choose numbers to write on each part of the target (figure 7.10a). Throw three small buttons/pegs/bits of paper onto the target. What's your total score? Play against someone else. What are all the possible scores?

FAVOURITE NUMBER

Choose a number that's special to you (figure 7.10b). Use a calculator and/or your head to write down as much as you can about how to make your number.

Many activities can be offered in an open enough way for children of a wide range of abilities to respond appropriately. 'Targets', for example, can be played with scores of one, two and three right up to scores of nine, ninety-nine and 999! Giving children the choice of what numbers to use can open up many existing pupil-book activities.

Another way to engage the mathematical thinking of the child in standard, closed, pupil-book activities is to ask them to create a similar page for someone else to do. For example, creating a page of simple subtractions will require that the child understands or discovers that the larger number must be written first (unless they are to get involved in negative numbers!).

In summary, you can make the best use of existing pupils' materials in mathematics by:

- making sure that it leads to practical activity wherever appropriate (e.g. pictures of farm animals becoming real toy farm animals on the desk);
- making the activity as personal and related to the child's real life as possible (e.g. a picture of a child going shopping with 10p to buy pictures of items becoming the pupils themselves visiting your own class shop, choosing and recording in their own way what they could buy);

- removing specific numbers and allowing children to choose for themselves;
- suggesting that pupils become 'authors' for a while and create similar pages for each other (and mark each other's, too).

Finally, it often makes very little difference what order some of the activities or exercises in pupils' books are done in, especially when you've adapted them to bring more Using and Applying into them as described here. So allow children some freedom to choose the order of activities wherever possible, and be alert to any of the children's own ideas for adapting and exploring activities. They must know that it's OK to make changes to an activity if they can see something interesting to explore. (Activities printed in books should not be thought of as sacrosanct.) For example, Joe was exploring his 'favourite number', 9, when he discovered that 3 + 3 + 3 made 9. He suddenly wanted to know what 2 + 2 + 2 would be, and 4 + 4 + 4, etc. so 9 was abandoned in favour of this new, self-invented activity. He even went on to notice that the number 3 was appearing as the pattern in his results:

$$1 + 1 + 1 = 3 \qquad\qquad 4 + 4 + 4 = 12$$
$$2 + 2 + 2 = 6 \qquad\qquad 5 + 5 + 5 = 15$$
$$3 + 3 + 3 = 9 \qquad\qquad 6 + 6 + 6 = 18$$

etc.

This linked right back to his initial fascination for 3 + 3 + 3 and he wrote:

$$3 \qquad +3 \qquad\qquad 12 \qquad +3$$
$$6 \qquad +3 \qquad\qquad 15 \qquad +3$$
$$9 \qquad +3 \qquad\qquad 18 \qquad +3$$

etc.

I cannot emphasise enough that Joe was not an exceptional child. *All* children show similar intrigue and interest in the way numbers behave when *they* are in control of the exploring, as is demonstrated by the CAN project (see page 25).

TYPES OF ACTIVITY

After having dispensed with pages of sums and other exercises of consolidation and practice, the mainstay of mathematical activity becomes:

- games;
- puzzles;

- investigations;
- problems

(whether in books or not).

Each of these could be practical, imaginary, verbal and/or recorded on paper. The recording, where appropriate, can be on worksheets, in class books, for displays, etc. and should mostly show the children's own ideas and methods of working. The consolidation and practice is embedded within these types of activity. Each type of activity already involves a purpose for doing it (e.g. to solve the problem, to play the game, etc.) which drives the learning, and hopefully the child's interest and motivation too. (Mathematics should never be done just to please the teacher or because the teacher or book insists on it.) Examples of these types of activity (for calculating) are:

Games

COUNT TO TWENTY

A game for two players. Start at 1. Take turns to count on up a number line either one or two places. So if the game has reached 6, you can either say 7 or 8. Whoever gets to 20 first wins. Which numbers are good to land on? Can you always win?

Try different end numbers; or try counting on one, two or three places.

THREE IN A ROW

1	2	3	4
5		7	8
9	10	11	12
13	14	15	16

FIGURE 7.11 *Three In A Row*

A game for two people (figure 7.11). You will need a die and about sixteen counters of two colours. Throw the die three times and record the numbers, e.g. 4, 3, 2. Choose how to combine them with addition and subtraction in order to capture a number on the grid, for example:

$$4 + 3 + 2 = 9$$
$$4 - 3 + 2 = 3$$
$$2 + 3 - 4 = 1$$

Place your colour of counter on your captured square. The winner is the first to get three squares in a row.

Try arranging numbers differently; or choosing different or repeating numbers; or changing the rules for winning.

Other games for calculation already mentioned:

'Around the track' (page 131)
'Pairs' (page 135)
'Singing games' (pages 72 and 86)
'Targets' (page 139)

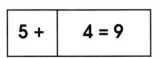

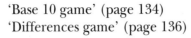

FIGURE 7.12 *Jigsaw Sums*

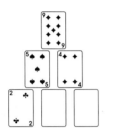

FIGURE 7.13 *Pyramid of Cards*

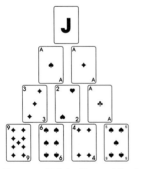

FIGURE 7.14 *Pyramid of Differences*

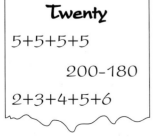

FIGURE 7.15 *Doodle Board*

'Base 10 game' (page 134)
'Differences game' (page 136)

and, of course, many well-known card games, dominoes and board games. (Although board games involve counting on and counting back, it can be useful to ask the children to adapt the rules so that more explicit calculating is required.) Given some 'numerical' equipment (such as dice, dominoes, spinners, number cards, etc.) the children themselves can invent their own games of calculation. This can be a mathematics topic in itself (see Games and Puzzles, pages 69–70).

Puzzles

SECRET NUMBER

'I've thought of a number. I've added 2 and got 17. What was my number?'

'I've thought of a number. I've subtracted 5 and got 1. What was my number?'

'I've thought of a number. The difference between it and 25 is 5. What was my number?'
(Two possible answers of course!)

JIGSAW SUMS

Each child writes about five sums on strips of paper and cuts each one into two (or three) pieces (figure 7.12). The pieces are jumbled and then swapped with a partner. Then they try to put them together.

PYRAMID OF CARDS

Using the ace as 1, can you build a pyramid where every card is the sum of the two cards below it (figure 7.13).

Try using the joker for zero; using Jack, Queen, King for 11, 12 and 13; using red cards for positive numbers and black cards for negative numbers; building a pyramid of differences where every card is the number difference between the two cards below (figure 7.14).

Investigations

DOODLE BOARD

Pin up a huge piece of paper. Choose a suitable number to write at the top. Everyone tries to contribute as many different ways as possible to make the number (figure 7.15).

MONEY, MONEY!

Find as many ways as possible to make 5p with real coins.

Write down your ideas, e.g. 2p + 2p + 1p. Try it for other amounts.

HOW DO I DO IT?

Draw a grid like the one in figure 7.16 on a large sheet of paper. choose your own number to go in the centre. Write down as many ways as you can to make your chosen number. Think carefully about how you work each one out so that you can write it in the correct space. (You may like to work with someone else.)

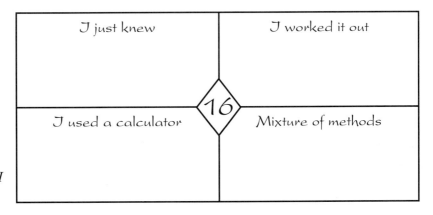

FIGURE 7.16 *'How Do I Do It' grid*

SUM SURVEY

Choose a sum that you think you can do in your head. Do it in your head and write down how you did it.

e.g.

14 + 15
10 + 10 + 4 + 5
20 + 9
29

or

14 + 15
14 + 5 = 19
19 + 10 = 29

Ask some other people to do the same sum in their heads.

Ask each person how they did it. Record some different ways to do the same calculation.

ADD NINE

Write down a long list of numbers. Add 9 to every number. Is there a pattern when you add 9? Try subtracting 9 from a long list of numbers greater than 10; or try adding a different number to your whole list.

It is absolutely essential that children explore their own ideas and their own thinking when doing an investigation. You can suggest ideas and offer possible ways forward, but it is the child who must decide. You cannot lead them along a path that only you can see; you can but stand behind them, point out some possible routes and let them decide which way to go.

Investigations are an extremely powerful way to learn about mathematics, especially in number work. A bank of starting points to explore numbers is far more important than any 'formal' number work. Within the CAN project (see page 25), teachers and children had to invent and share a lot of these starting points for themselves because there is such a severe lack of provision for this in published materials. Other investigations for calculating already mentioned are:

'Domino squares' (page 135)
'Snake of triangles' (page 11)
'Show a sum' (page 24)
'Shape sums' (page 25)
'Scrap paper' (page 157)
'Number facts display' (page 134)
'Hunt for twos' (page 137)

There is a difference between an investigation and an investigatory approach to learning. Children can explore (i.e. investigate) possibilities within games, puzzles and problems. An investigation sets a context for pure exploration, for its own sake, and not towards any end result. This is why so many teachers really find them difficult to accept into their teaching. You cannot teach in the sense of leading the child to an objective or goal. You can only 'facilitate the learning' and enjoy the surprises of where it might lead.

Problems

TIN OF MONEY
For example, school trip money, dinner money, collections. Find out how much money is in the tin. Find a way to check your total.

CALCULATOR CRISIS
Pretend that one of the number keys on your calculator won't work. Write some numbers that use the broken key. Find a way to do them on your calculator, e.g. My 5 won't work. 15 + 5 could be 14 + 1 + 4 + 1 or 14 + 6.

ONE, TWO, THREE, FOUR …
Try to make all the numbers to 20 (or 100) using only the digits 1, 2, 3 and 4. For example, 16 could be 14 + 2; 58 could be 34 + 24.

COLOUR-CODED NUMBERS

Make up a secret colour code for the digits 0 to 9 (figure 7.17).
Make up some colour sums for someone else (which include all
the answers) (figure 7.18).

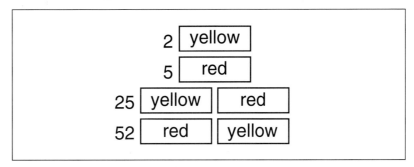

FIGURE 7.17 *Colour Code*

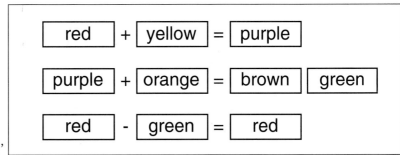

FIGURE 7.18 *Colour 'Sums'*

Swap sums and try to crack each other's code.

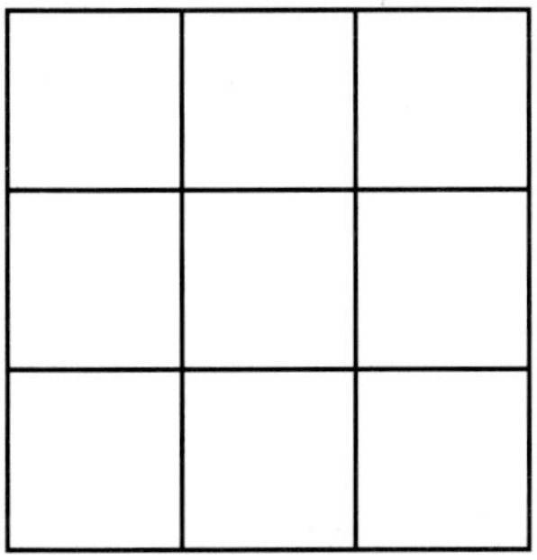

MAGIC SQUARES

Put the digits 1 to 9 in these squares (figure 7.19) so that each
line of three, including diagonals, adds up to 15.

SHOPPING

Either real or pretend play shopping will present numerical
problems to solve in working out how to pay for items and how
much change, etc.

FIGURE 7.19 *Magic
Square Grid*

HOW MANY DAYS?

… until Christmas? Easter? the weekend? your birthday? end of
term? half term? (anything topical or special to the child).
Provide a calendar and a calculator.

Problems for children to solve, whether real or imagined, must
always allow for many different approaches. The children need to
decide what calculations are required and choose and use their
own methods for doing them. Finally, they need to check and
consider whether the results are sensible. These things can all be

done in a variety of ways, and it is the variety that needs to be shared and developed, not specific outcomes.

Numerical problems present themselves often in daily school life and can be seized upon to explore the variety of children's approaches to them (see section A). Other numerical problems already mentioned are:

'Arithmagons' (page 111)
'Consecutive number results' (page 115)
'Shoe-box shopping' (page 137)
'Crayons' (page 137)
'PE equipment' (page 137)
'How many petals?' (page 137)
'Hymn books', etc. and other problems taken from children's own surroundings (page 137)
Solving real problems (section A) (page 41)

Solving numerical problems often works best at Key Stage 1 when the children work in pairs of similar ability, and have some choice about the problems they tackle.

OTHER CONTEXTS FOR MATHEMATICS ACTIVITIES

General class topics can sometimes provide purposeful contexts for mathematics activities, and it is worth considering what aspects of the Programmes of Study could be involved. For example:

- A class topic on bears could include some measuring and numerical problem solving in organising a teddy-bears' picnic.
- A topic on newspapers could provide a context for calculating how many articles can fit on the page depending on the number of words and sizes of any pictures.
- A topic on birds might offer opportunities to calculate how many of certain types of birds visit the playground over several days, adding together the results from different children, or looking at differences between days.

The calculating will mostly occur as something to serve another purpose (e.g. quantities and costs for the picnic, making up the newspaper or learning about the habits of birds). 'Dressing up' calculating, in contrast, has little or no purpose (e.g. 'three birds have ... legs', or 'bears cost 20p. How many can you buy for £1?').

All the 'hidden mathematics curriculum' (section A) can provide ideas for activities related to your theme, and sometimes it is extremely helpful to bring such ideas explicitly into your mathematics curriculum time. For example, for calculating:

EXAMPLES OF CALCULATING IN THE HIDDEN MATHEMATICS CURRICULUM		
Chapter 3: **Class** **Projects**	'Voting and checking' 'Slices of bread' 'Devising rotas' 'Star coins'	page 36 page 38 page 42 page 50
Chapter 4: **Everyday** **Activities**	'Register time' 'Collecting money' 'How many days until…' 'Birthdays' 'Getting changed' 'Getting into groups' 'Lining up' 'Pretend meal' 'Shopping' 'Singing' 'Cooking' 'Home time'	page 52 page 53 page 58 page 59 page 63 page 64 page 65 page 68 page 71 page 72 page 73 page 76
Chapter 5: **Other areas of** **the curriculum**	'Number songs' 'Would you rather'	page 86 page 88

Finally, there are activities to be drawn from recorded mathematics television programmes (with their related follow-up suggestions), computer programs, programmable toys and any other available new technology (e.g. videodisk).

CONCLUSION

Pages of sums have very little to offer in terms of mathematical thinking. But some of the alternative activities offered do use sums, written in the formal way, e.g. $3 + 5 = 8$ within games, puzzles, investigations and problems. So how will young children learn what they are in the first place? The calculator is the most obvious place to meet the symbols of $+$, $-$, $=$, etc. Most children will have played with a calculator alongside the many different types of activities that introduce the concepts of adding and subtracting to them. Whenever they record their calculator work their recording will start to look just like traditional sums. (Formal symbols should always be slipped in almost unnoticed like this, and should never be the starting point in trying to build understanding.) (See chapter 2, page 18.)

Mathematical activities can be adapted from existing resources or developed using the range of contexts described. Devices such as 'naughty teddies' or 'close your eyes' (whilst something is changed) or deliberately misunderstanding something that was imprecise can help young children to enjoy things going wrong and empower them to see the mathematics in putting it right.

The best activities for mathematical thinking will be the ones that are developed using the children's own ideas or those that are open-ended enough to allow the children to make some of their own choices and decisions.

CHAPTER 8 MATHEMATICAL MOMENTS

This chapter includes:
- Games
- Action songs
- Counting games
- Activities
- Puzzles
- Mental imagery
- Conclusion

This chapter offers a collection of games, songs, activities, puzzles and mental imagery that can be done in five or ten minutes with a group or whole class anywhere and anytime (e.g. on the carpet, while lining up, waiting, travelling, etc.). There are a variety of ideas covering many aspects of mathematics at different levels, organised by type of activity. These mathematical moments could be used selectively alongside specific themes, but are offered as a miscellany of ideas to use informally whenever you happen to find yourself with a few minutes to spare.

GAMES

SIMON SAYS

Play this using vocabulary of position and movement, number ideas, shapes and measures. For example:

- Simon Says put your hands *on* your head, *inside* your jumper, *above* your head, *under* your bottom, *behind* your back, *next to* each other ...
- Simon Says make your nose move in a *straight* line, in a *zig-zag* line, in a *circle*, etc., *turn* your head as far as you can one way, now the other way ...
- Simon Says show me *three* fingers, *seven* fingers, *twenty-three* fingers (children can get together!), *four more than one* finger, *two fewer than five* fingers, no fingers at all *(zero)*!

- Simon Says make a *square* shape with your fingers, a *circle*, an *oblong*, a *narrower oblong*, a *triangle*, a *different triangle*, etc.
- Simon Says put your hands *as far away from* your nose as possible: put your head *as close to* your toes as possible: make your smile *as wide* as possible; put your toes *as high* as possible; make your arms *as long* as you can …

Don't forget to catch them out from time to time when Simon *didn't* say to do it. (Children don't need to be 'out', they can always continue to play.) Try letting various children have a go at inventing mathematical Simon Says.

GUESS THE PERSON
- 'I've thought of a person. I can only answer 'yes' or 'no' to your questions. Can you find out who it is?'

The person could be someone in the class, an adult in school, a famous person, a story character, a baby, Father Christmas, etc. – anyone as long as everyone knows him/her. Children should develop their questioning skills/using classifications such as:

- male/female;
- adult/child;
- famous/not famous;
- real/imaginary (careful about Father Christmas!);
- comes into school or not.

Wild guesses should be discouraged and good questions reinforced. You may also need to summarise the criteria they've discovered from time to time (e.g. 'You know now that it's a boy, he doesn't come to this school, he's younger than you …').

PEEP A SHAPE
Use a large book or something to be a screen. Let a tiny part of a shape peep out from behind the screen.

- 'What might it be?'
- 'What could it be?'
- 'What else could it be?'
- 'What do you know that it isn't?'

(This part of the game is much more important than what the shape actually is.) Either show a bit more of the shape or hide it and let a different part of the shape peep.

- 'Now what do you think it might be?'
- Try using different resources for the shapes (e.g. plastic shapes, cards, logi blocs, etc.). You could also use three-dimensional shapes, or you could try it with numbers instead (on cards or from puzzle sets).

I SPY

'I spy with my little eye something ...

- which is square shaped;
- which has a triangle on it;
- which is spherical (like a ball);
- which has a circle on the end;
- where there are five of them together;
- with a two on it;
- where there are eight;
- shorter than my finger;
- thicker than this book;
- lower than the shelf, etc.

The children themselves should take turns to do a mathematical 'I Spy' once they understand the idea.

FIZZ BUZZ

The children should be arranged in sequence (e.g. in rows, in a circle). Everyone says a counting number in turn, in order, but no one is allowed to say any number with a three in it; they have to say 'fizz' instead: one, two, fizz, four, five ... twelve, fizz, fourteen, etc.

Once the children have got the idea, then any number with a seven in it has to be replaced by 'buzz' as well: ... four, five, six, buzz, eight ... fifteen, sixteen, buzz, eighteen, etc.

Any number with both three and seven, or with extra threes or sevens, has to be said with extra fizzes and buzzes, so thirty-seven is 'fizz-buzz', seventy-three is 'buzz-fizz', thirty-three is 'fizz-fizz' and seventy-seven is 'buzz-buzz'.

See if you can all get to 100 without a mistake! Every time a mistake is made, it must be corrected very quickly or else you have to go back to the beginning. Be careful when you get to the thirties and seventies! To make the game more challenging, try inventing other words for other numbers (e.g. 'fuzz' for four) or try counting backwards from twenty or 100.

GUESS MY NUMBER/SHAPE

This is a variation on *Guess the Person*, using mathematical items instead. The questions will need to focus on the properties of numbers and shapes. For example:

- 'Has it got any curves?'
- 'Has it got square corners?' } Shape
- 'Is it a 3D shape?'

- 'Is it bigger than fifty?'
- 'Has it got a two in it?' } Number
- 'Is it even?'

Sometimes it helps to define the set of shapes or numbers beforehand, e.g. 'I've chosen one of these shapes' or 'I've chosen a number between one and twenty-five (or one and 100)'.

I WENT TO THE SUPERMARKET

Go round the class with this sentence: 'I went shopping and had …… in my trolley'.

Each person has to repeat the sequence of all the items that are in the trolley so far and then choose something to put in themselves at the end (e.g. 'I went shopping and had sausages, bread, cereals, honey and … in my trolley.') When you have all got as far as you can go, try saying 'I didn't have my money, so I had to put it all back.' Then try taking turns to go backwards, repeating the sequence as it gets shorter and shorter until everything is put back! (The ideas of inverses and sequences are an important part of mathematics.) You could just put three or four things into the trolley for the first few times you play.

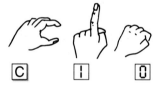

FIGURE 8.1 *Calculator Fingers Game*

CALCULATOR FINGERS

This is a variation on Paper, Stone, Scissors. Children play in pairs (opposite each other). They both choose to make their fingers into a C (for cancel), 1 or 0 behind their backs (figure 8.1). After a count of three, they show what they've chosen and see who wins:

- 1 beats 0 (because it's bigger).
- C beats 1 (because it cancels it).
- 0 beats C (because it can't be cancelled).

The mathematical logic of this game is intriguing: that whatever you choose, it can win or lose depending on what it's compared to. Children usually love it and will play for ages.

HANGMAN

For this, you need coloured cubes and pencil and paper. Instead of guessing the letters to make a word, children play in pairs to discover the colours of a rod of five cubes, as follows:

- Fit five coloured cubes into a rod.
- Hide it (in your lap, behind a book, etc.).
- Your partner guesses a colour at a time.
- If you've got the colour, say where it is, e.g. 'Yes. It's on the end.', 'Yes. There are two that colour, one in the middle and the other next to it'.

- If not, then you draw one part of the hangman. (Instead of a hangman, you could simply give them ten 'lives' or chances.)
- The guesser has some cubes to build the same rod as the game continues.
- Check that they're the same at the end.

WHAT'S IN MY POCKET?

Secretly put a classroom object in your pocket (or into a 'feely bag'). The group have just twenty questions to discover what it is.

THE TURNING GAME

FIGURE 8.2 *The Turning Game*

Two children stand at the front. Other children take turns to offer instructions to turn either a quarter turn, a half turn or a three-quarter turn to the child's left or right, first to one child and then to the other (figure 8.2).

If they ever both face the same way, they have to sit down and two more children have a go. (If the children notice that it doesn't matter which way they turn for a half turn, then they can just say 'half turn' instead.)

Alternatively, try it with three children standing at the front. If any two end up facing the same way, they are out. (This is much harder to avoid.) Then try it with four children all facing different ways to start. There will have to be two children out every time, unless they use whole turns! (Let the children discover this as they play.) Invent other rules. For example, anyone facing front is 'safe' and can't be out.

ACTION SONGS

THE HOKEY COKEY

'You put your left arm in, your left arm out ...' This well-known song helps children to learn right and left, but beware that in a circle, they will see the children opposite them seemingly using the other arm or leg. This is worth commenting on: 'That's strange! It looks as if you're using different arms/legs. Let's check ... Why is it like that?'

MIMING IN ACTION SONGS

Many songs can progressively involve more and more miming until there is no singing left, e.g. In a Cottage in a Wood; One Finger, One Thumb Keep Moving; Head, Shoulders, Knees and Toes, etc.

SINGING NUMBERS

Take any song that the children know well and sing it with numbers in order instead of words. For example, Baa Baa Black

Sheep ended up at twenty-one when we tried it. See what numbers you can get to with different songs. Which song might get to a number greater than thirty?

More ideas for singing are on page 72 under 'Everyday Activities'.

COUNTING GAMES

SILENT COUNTING

'I'm going to count silently. Tell me to stop when you think I've got to the number we agreed'

- 'How close were you?'
- 'How fast are we counting?'
- 'I'll count at this speed ... Let's try again.'

You can try this with many different numbers (let the children choose) and different agreed counting speeds. Alternatively, try counting backwards from certain numbers, or choose various children to come and do the silent counting instead of you. You say 'stop' when you think they are at an agreed target number. Or try starting counting from different numbers.

EGG-TIMER COUNTING

Ask the children how many they think they can count to before the timer runs out. Then try counting faster or slower. 'If we count at this speed, where do you think we'd get to?' Try estimating after the timer has started:

'Whoops, it's already going. What do you think now?'

CIRCLE COUNTING

Stand in a circle (with a small group) and choose a number (e.g. three). Count round and round the circle with every third person sitting down. Keep going with the ones that are still standing.

Who will be the last person left standing? Try to predict it several times during the counting: 'Who's it going to be?!' Then try it again, starting with someone else. Try it with a different number. (Any number is good to try, even a much higher number. One is interesting too!)

COUNTING PATTERNS

Try counting together, quite slowly, in:

- ones (from different starting points, and backwards);
- twos (from different starting points – it always makes the same two distinct patterns);

- fives (and backwards);
- tens (and from different starting numbers, e.g. two, twelve, twenty-two, etc.);
- hundreds, thousands and even millions (young children love those huge numbers, and it's really only like counting in ones!);
- halves and quarters.

Sometimes it helps children to start these patterns by whispering the missed-out numbers, or tapping the floor for each unspoken number. They shouldn't be under any pressure to join in; some children need to just listen to the rhythms and patterns, joining in when they are ready.

COUNTING CONSTANTS

Make two very simple cards (or write onto a board and point to the one you want) (figure 8.3a).

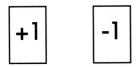

FIGURE 8.3A *Card controlled counting*

Start with any number (a child can choose). The children need to watch the cards carefully to know which one to use and be ready to change their counting as soon as the other card is shown, e.g. fifteen, sixteen, seventeen (change card), sixteen, fifteen, fourteen (change card), fifteen, sixteen, etc.

Then include two more cards (figure 8.3b) so that you can all get stuck on a number, e.g. fourteen, thirteen, twelve (change card), twelve, twelve, twelve, etc., before carrying on again!

FIGURE 8.3B

- Try it with +2 and −2 as well.
- Let it go below zero (or discuss what to do when they need to go below zero).
- Have a target number. If you hit it, the game ends or starts again. (It can be fun to use the cards to make the counting go close to the target number and just escape in time!)

TENS AND ONES

'Sometimes when we're counting, we'll switch to counting in tens and then back to ones, so be ready for the switch' (figure 8.4).

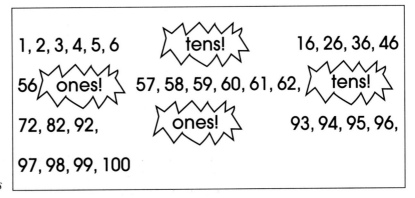

FIGURE 8.4 *Tens and Ones*

Count quite slowly and enjoy a bit of a pause, building up to each change-over. Try to get to 100.

- Let individual children have to go at calling tens and ones (see if they can get everyone to 100).
- Try counting backwards in tens and ones.
- If possible, include counting in hundreds as well and try to get up to 1000.

ACTIVITIES

EXERCISES, EXERCISES

'Exercises, Exercises,
See me do my exercises!'

Repeat this over and over, rhythmically. Using your two index fingers only, make them extend and retract in time to the rhythm, vertically first, then horizontally, then alternating (e.g. vertical, horizontal, vertical, horizontal, etc.) and finally try to make one finger go vertically whilst the other is going horizontally, and alternate that!

REFLECTIONS

Each child has an 'imaginary mirror'. Everything that one hand does, the other has to do the reflection of it. Move slowly.

- Try going nearer/further away from the 'mirror'.
- Make shapes with your fingers.
- Turn your hands in opposite directions.
- Try drawing in the air with index fingers and reflect it as it's happening (like using sparklers to draw patterns outside on a dark night).

FINGER PLAY

- 'Show me five fingers … in another way … and another way'
- 'Show me any number that is *not* five. Let's check … no fives anywhere. We've got an eight, a two … I hope I don't find a five anywhere.'
- Try other 'not' numbers.
- Try 'no numbers more than five' (or fewer than).
- Try making shapes in different ways (an oval, a heart shape, a semicircle, a diamond, etc.) and inventing unusual shapes (and describing them).

DRAW ON MY BACK

In pairs, children can take turns to draw a number or a shape onto their partner's back using their finger. Their partner tries to guess what it was after feeling it.

- 'Draw it slowly and carefully. Can you feel it? What number/shape do you think it is?'

CLAPPING RHYTHMS

'Join in the rhythm when you can. Listen and watch for when it changes.

- Clap, Clap, Slap, Clap, Clap, Slap …
- Finger touch, Clap, Clap, Clap, Finger touch, Clap, Clap, Clap …

- Clap, Clap, Stamp, Stamp, Shh! Clap, Clap, Stamp, Stamp, Shh! Children are good at inventing rhythms and patterns like these. Let different children have a go at leading it.

ESTIMATING ACTIVITIES

Almost any object could be picked up fairly quickly and the children invited to estimate something about it: e.g. How long is it? About how many cubes long? How heavy is it? (Pass it round.) About how many conkers would balance it? How many are in here? How much would this hold? How many capfuls or pentop-fuls or thimble-fuls?

SCRAP PAPER

Everyone needs a piece of scrap paper; it doesn't matter what shape, size or colour or whether it's been written on (it could even be a piece from a waste-paper bin), but it must *not* have been folded.

- Make one fold and open it out. (What shapes have you got? How many parts? Are they halves?)
- Make another fold and open it out again. (What shapes now? Are they all the same? How many parts? Is it the same for everyone?) (figure 8.5)

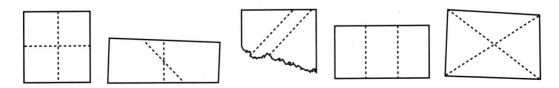

FIGURE 8.5 *Scrap Paper folding*

- Try making a curved fold. Is it possible?
- Try predicting and testing how many tears you'd need to do to rip it into four pieces.

OPPOSITES

'Whatever I do, you do the opposite.' For example:

- Stretch up tall ... children crouch down small.
- Face the window ... they face the wall.
- Show ten fingers ... they show none at all.
- Make them all spikey ... they make them into a ball, etc.

(Somethings you do will have several possible ways to show opposites! Discuss any variety.)

PUZZLES

NUMBER SEARCH

Ask some children (about five or six) to stand up so that everyone can see them. 'I can see three of something. What is it?' (e.g. girls, rings, pairs of shoes with laces, etc.).

- Try other numbers.
- Let the children take turns to 'see a number' and everyone else has to find out what it is.

ROBOT HEAD

'Give me a number. Thank you. I'll put it in my robot head (in one ear, whirry noises, out the other ear). Here it comes ... It's changed! It's ...... now. Give me another number (repeat the process). 'What does my robot head do to numbers?'

- Try a child being a robot head instead of you.
- Try numbers changing in different ways. The robot head could, for example, add one to every number; cancel numbers (eat them up!); add a hundred to every number; halve every number.

WHISPERED CHANGES

Choose children to come to you one at a time. Whisper something they must do as they walk behind your back and go back to their place. Everyone watches several children do this, and tries to work out what's happening. Examples of some whispered changes:

- fold your arms;
- scratch your head;

- pretend to trip up;
- giggle;
- stretch your fingers;
- hiccup;
- put your hands behind your back;
- walk up really straight;
- look happy/sad/cross.

The idea is that children need to see several 'inputs and outputs' before they will be able to work out what's happening. So the changes shouldn't be too obvious.

GUESS THE PICTURE

Draw a picture slowly on the board (or wherever all the children can see). They must try to guess what it's going to be as you draw. Try it with shapes (figure 8.6a and b):

FIGURE 8.6a   *Guess the Shape*

FIGURE 8.6b

Try it with numbers (figure 8.7a) or calculator digits (figure 8.7b):

FIGURE 8.7a   *Guess the Number*

FIGURE 8.7b

Or larger numbers (figure 8.7c):

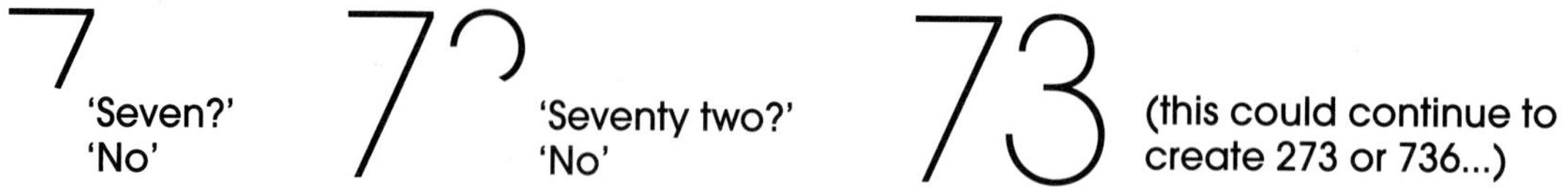

7 'Seven?'
'No'

72 'Seventy two?'
'No'

73 (this could continue to create 273 or 736...)

FIGURE 8.7c

THE DIFFERENCE IS...

'I've thought of two numbers. The difference between them is two. What were my numbers?'

- Try with differences of one, ten, three, etc.
- Play it like twenty questions, finding out where the numbers are (e.g. 'Are they less than ten?').

CLUES

'I'm thinking of a number. I'll give you some clues about it until you can guess what it is. It's a two digit number. It's larger than fifty. The two digits are the same. They don't have any straight lines in them.' 'Sixty-six!' 'No' 'Eighty-eight?' 'Yes.'

- Try allowing a few guesses after each clue. (The children will appreciate that it gets easier with more clues.)
- Try letting individual children think of a number and give clues.
- Try it with shapes (e.g. it's got four sides, two sides are longer than the other ones, etc.)

MENTAL IMAGERY

BIG AND SMALL

'Close your eyes and imagine the biggest thing you can think of ...'

- Hear some children's ideas: 'Which is the smallest out of these two big things? Is it small or big?'
- Try imagining the smallest thing possible. Which is the biggest small thing? Is it big or small?
- Try it for: longest/shortest, heaviest/lightest, widest/narrowest, deepest/shallowest, furthest away/nearest.

HALVES

'Imagine that you can cut anything in half. What would half of some of these things look like?' (figure 8.8)

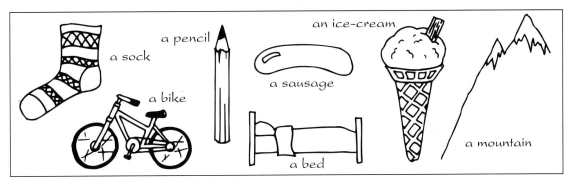

FIGURE 8.8 *Imagining Halves*

- 'Where would you cut?'
- 'Why?'
- 'Is there another way to cut in half?'
- 'Do the two halves have to be the same size and/or shape?'

NUMBERS

FIGURE 8.9 *Imagining Numbers*

'Imagine three of something.'

- 'What did everyone imagine?'
- 'How different a number of things can look!'
- Try imagining different numbers of things (including zero!).

FLOATING IN SPACE

'Imagine some numbers floating in space around you (close your eyes).'

- 'What numbers can you see?'
- 'Are they in order?'
- 'What are they doing?'
- 'Are they coloured?'
- 'How are they moving?'
- 'What are they made of?'

TALKING NUMBERS

Make two groups of children. Give each group a number. The

numbers are going to argue with each other about their importance (and then decide to be friends afterwards). 'What might you say to each other?' For example:

15 I'm more important than you because I'm bigger!
10 Yes but I'm the very first two digit number
15 You've just got zero as one of your digits!
10 That's what makes me special you fool … I can be added to any number so easily!

And now friends:

15 Oh, come on, let's go and play twenty fives.
10 No, I've got a better idea. Put your five down and we can play twins.

Some of these arguments and conversations will work very well whilst children get stuck on others. Just move on to try another number of the children's choosing. (Their imaginations for this are far better than ours usually, and often explore their understanding and knowledge of numbers.)

SPIDERS

Imagine that you are a tiny spider crawling over a hundred square.

- 'Which numbers are you crawling over?' (It might help to have a hundred square on show for the first few times you do this.)
- See if the children can follow each other's described paths/routes.
- 'Try walking in a square shape. Which numbers do you tread on?'
- 'What about an oblong-shaped path?'
- 'A zig-zag path?'
- 'A spiralling path?'
- 'What about marching along lines?'
- 'Stop and have a rest. What number are you on?'

CONCLUSION

These informal moments can help enormously for developing personal qualities or attitudes towards mathematics. Mistakes and things going wrong can be associated with mathematics and enjoyed because it doesn't matter: 'Oh, dear! Let's try that again! How can we make it easier?!' Using children's imaginations is a particularly powerful way to bring mathematics into their minds, and hearing that so many people imagine things in different ways

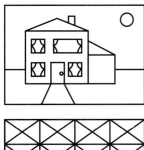

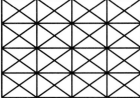

FIGURE 8.10 *Colouring Challenge*

can broaden understanding and build confidence.

The ideas offered here are teacher-led. But you could also build up a box of easily accessible games, puzzles, problems and investigations as 'holding activities' that children can pick up and use themselves whenever they have a few moments to spare. This is a good place for some of those logical reasoning activities that don't seem to fit under mathematics 'content' headings, or themes. For example, draw a picture or pattern with regions to colour in (figure 8.10). What is the fewest number of colours you can use to colour it in with no two regions of the same colour touching each other (except corner to corner)? NB You could have some ready to do in the box.

The children can be encouraged to invent or contribute ideas that they think are suitable (and intriguing or simply enjoyable) to go into your class's 'Puzzle Box'.

SUMMING UP SECTION B

In summary, the key features of planning your mathematics curriculum time are as follows.

CHOOSING A THEME

Consider previous themes and general topics in order to achieve a balanced coverage of the Programmes of Study over time.

CREATING A SET OF ACTIVITIES

Include a variety of types and ways of working, and any 'extras', like fun days, events, ideas from the hidden mathematics curriculum, displays, etc.

SELECTING DAILY (OR WEEKLY) ACTIVITIES

Match suitable choices of activities to various individuals, pairs, groups or whole class.

To take account of children's developing interests and ideas, your plans for mathematics can – and should – change quite frequently. In order to be flexible enough to respond to their initiatives, you will need to:

- recognize that, because they are the children's initiatives, progression in learning will be more secure than following the page-by-page 'progression' imposed within many published schemes;
- have a bank of resources and ideas from which to draw at relatively short notice;
- be prepared to go into the unknown and be surprised by the mathematics that you and the children find there.

CONCLUSION

This section includes:

CHAPTER 9

WAYS FORWARD

This chapter includes:
- Ways forward to develop your teaching of Using and Applying mathematics
- Ways forward to develop attitudes to learning
- Ways forward to develop planning and organisation
- Ways forward to develop assessment and evaluation
- Ways forward to develop communication with parents

'… it is not enough to teach them to read, write and count; you must also teach them to read between the lines, that is, to reflect, to think for themselves.'

(Emilie Carles (1900–1979) from
A Wild Herb Soup: The Life of a French Countrywoman)

Accept that you cannot ever do everything that you'd like to do for the children in your class. Get used to making priorities in the short and long term so that you know *when* you can develop those things that are most important to you. Be creative in tackling problems. Don't be afraid to ask colleagues, friends, or the children themselves for their ideas. Jot down all sorts of possibilities, however extreme or surprising. Don't ever be defeated. Enjoy the process of trial and error in attempting to find solutions. Know that what works today may not work tomorrow, and what works with these children may not work with the next group. Constantly and informally reflect on all you do. Good teaching will be forever challenging.

'Procrastinators are afraid. Of change, of failure, even success.'

(Eve Pascoe, SHE magazine, 1994)

You will never be able to develop your teaching of mathematics to incorporate Using and Applying by reading this book or any other book, or by watching someone else do it. You have to have the courage to have a go at something like it *for yourself* with *your class*.

Copying the ideas in this book, using the words as a script to follow, would only ever be a diluted, second-hand version. Make it your own. Take one or two aspects of an idea that can be built or adapted onto your way of teaching and try that. This book is intended to be used as inspiration for new ways for yourself.

WAYS FORWARD TO DEVELOP YOUR TEACHING OF USING AND APPLYING MATHEMATICS

- Stop giving answers for a day, to anything! Find ways to help the children find out for themselves or to check their own work;
- Focus on your questions for a day. Make them as open as possible.

'Studies have consistently shown that the typical classroom teacher asks factual, convergent questions more frequently than divergent ones.'

(Cornelius and Casler, 1991)

Try to stop yourself from leading children's thinking your way with your questions – try to find out how *they* are thinking and prompt them to try out *their* ideas.

- Take one activity, whether it's a page from a workbook or some other task, and devote some time to making it more open, e.g. allowing children to choose the numbers or to devise their own sheets for each other (see page 139).
- Try an investigation or problem with a pair of children, concentrating on helping them to explore their own ideas. Don't be afraid to offer it to children of lower ability.

'Many teachers are surprised to find that children they regard as being poor at maths excel at investigations.'

(Helen Walland 1993)

- Focus on the first strand of the Programme of Study for Using and Applying Mathematics – Making and monitoring decisions to solve problems – and talk about it with the children. Everyone is to look out for any examples of any of it during the day in all they do. (Go back to it from time to time to remind everyone what they're all looking for.)
- Observe a pair of children who are engrossed in their play. Jot down all the mathematical thinking that you see (see page 16);
- Have a 'brainstorming' session with the class (or a group) where everyone offers lots of possible ideas for an assembly, a

topic, a trip, a display, etc. Or share ideas for possible solutions to a class problem. Make use of some of the childrens ideas.

- Get together with a colleague (or two) and both try the same investigation, problem or game with children in your classes. Chat about the results afterwards.

- If possible, arrange to offer some mathematics to some children alongside a colleague. Plan it together and discuss it afterwards in terms of Using and Applying. (Choose something you can look forward to!)

- Try some 'real world' mathematics. For example, shopping or conducting a survey for a real purpose. Map all the mathematical experiences onto the Programmes of Study afterwards.

- Scribble down the questions that children ask you during one session. Share with them afterwards the types of questions they've asked. Focus on the best and worst ones in terms of independent learning.

- Make time to stand back, observe, listen, assess, reflect, enjoy, rest …

WAYS FORWARD TO DEVELOP ATTITUDES TO LEARNING

- Don't expect to achieve anything overnight. Think, instead, of 'training' the children to: think for themselves in school; make decisions; welcome mistakes and unknowns; listen to others. For example, stop all the children just to hear about someone who's had three different ideas of their own in trying to solve a problem which remains unsolved!

- Try offering choices between activities sometimes, so that the children have some control over what they do and/or what order they do it in.

- Swap work and play so that children know they are expected to concentrate and work hard at their play activities and explore and 'play' within their work.

'It is within [Early Years teachers'] power to encourage a feeling of fun and mutual discovery, but it is equally possible for them to create an atmosphere of dull drudgery where children's interests have to wait until adult-initiated tasks are completed, e.g. "you can play when you have done your work".'

(Early Years Curriculum Group)

- Start a new term with blank display boards and involve the children in creating their classroom. Ask them to bring various items from home to use as mathematics materials (e.g. lolly sticks, shells, boxes, etc.).

- Acknowledge that everyone has different ways of learning and offer a variety of types of activity for each aspect of mathematics. (Be careful that your own best ways of learning/working with mathematics don't dominate everything you offer the class.)
- Put mathematics into contexts that are as real and/or personal to the children as possible. Have real reasons or purposes for activities. Learning is then driven by the purpose rather than by you.
- Write down a list of the things you value most in other people. How many of those things do you do as a teacher for your pupils?
- When you go on INSET courses, how do you feel? (Humiliated? Bored? Critical? Excited? Relaxed? Thoughtful?) How do you expect to feel? How often do you go to something (e.g. a staff meeting) that really engages your interest, motivation and intellect? What was it that made it so good? Do you do any of that for your pupils?
- Show children that you are learning too. Young children love nothing more than seeing their teacher admitting to being wrong or not knowing something! Extend this to colleagues so that you can learn from each other.
  - Visit each other's classrooms.
  - Share children between classes sometimes.
  - Hold a 'things that went wrong' staff meeting.
  - Make things for other classes.
  - Come together and listen to what everyone does throughout the school to teach a small aspect of mathematics (e.g. fractions).
  - Invite teachers from pre-school and junior (or senior) teachers to join in with a mathematics staff meeting.

WAYS FORWARD TO DEVELOP PLANNING AND ORGANISING

- Try timetabling your teaching time so that you know what your priority is for each session, keeping the other things 'ticking over'.

'It helped me to know that, although I wanted to go to that group over there, it wasn't my priority and I would be able to get involved in their mathematics with them when they came back to it next session or next day.'

- Think about whether to timetable yourself for specific groups of children or particular curriculum areas.
- Plan collections of activities for each session where there will not be too much demand on you all at the same time. You may have to decide when, within each activity, you are likely to be needed most (if at all).
- Keep your plans as a cumulative record of what the children have experienced. Use a highlighter pen to show what you did and make comments/evaluations/assessments onto the used plans themselves.
- Make a collection of good 'holding activities' for mathematics so that children can do worthwhile activities without you (see page 163). Talk about them from time to time so that children know exactly what to do without asking.
- Consider planning across several years, for one year, for each term, half-term, each week, each day …

'For me, I use daily plans most because with very young children things change fast …'

'I'm always changing my plans and redressing the balance. I write a lot of it down. But I know Judy keeps most of it in her head …'

'It used to be far too free and easy. The National Curriculum moved us into too detailed a planning and recording, chopping up everything into tiny bits. Now we're moving back to a more sensible middle ground where planning is important (regularly), but is also highly flexible (*because* it is regular and frequent).'

- Think of planning as going shopping once a week or fortnight. Do a 'big shop', knowing roughly what you need, and then during the week you can pick and choose from all your ingredients to create a 'balanced diet' of mathematics, being able to accommodate spontaneous opportunities and new interests as they arise.
- Leave some 'gaps' in your planning so that children can contribute their ideas and so that you can have some space and time to spread into if necessary.
- Analyse what you do during one day. How much of the day are you interacting with children's intellect and learning (talking with them, listening to their ideas, etc.) and how much of the day are you organising them and solving procedural problems?
- Allow children to choose sometimes if they'd like to work on some mathematics with someone else or on their own.

Children have very different preferences within different types of activity.

- Young children seem to work well in pairs (or individually) without an adult. Don't be over-ambitious about groups of young children actually working together, unless the group is made up of a set of pairs or individuals doing different aspects of an activity. (You're welcome to prove me wrong, of course!)

WAYS FORWARD TO DEVELOP ASSESSMENT AND EVALUATION

- Ask individuals to reflect upon what *they* think they've learned, from time to time. Many young children are adept at describing their thinking in terms of *how* they worked, rather than focusing on particular outcomes.

'What do you think you've learned?'
'Well, I learned that you can estimate something and then when you're finding out you can have a better estimate getting closer and closer …'

(Mark, age six years, whilst finding out how many cupfuls filled the teapot, etc.)

- Explain sometimes what the purpose is of a set of activities (e.g. 'All these games and puzzles are to help us practice adding and subtracting in our heads'). Then you can focus on this (and other learning that may arise) more explicitly with the children.

'… children should know why they are doing any classroom activity, what its purpose is and what the teacher's expectations are.'

(Shirley Clarke, 1994)

- Except in rare circumstances, assessments can always be made during teaching and learning activities. If an aspect of mathematics is put into a variety of different contexts (and explored in any order), then any one of those contexts can serve to demonstrate that the child has understood the idea, once they have experienced some of the others.
- Plan some times of very low teacher input, when the teaching and learning activities are either continuing from an earlier input or simply don't require much teacher time. Use this time to discuss children's work with them, individually, making notes and observations about any obvious misunderstandings or any particular strengths.

- Use your marked planning sheets to evaluate coverage of aspects of mathematics. Look for any obvious gaps in the experiences children have been having so far.
- Think of children's learning of mathematics as exploring and getting to know and understand a whole region or territory of related ideas. Assessment then becomes an evaluation of how much of this experience they have had and how confident they are within it before moving them on to the next set of activities. Don't be too precise and detailed. Instead, get a general feeling of confidence.

'We have banks of activities in year 1 which are roughly organised into three stages. For example, number work is broken into:

i)   Pre-number
ii) Early Number
iii) Number

I find it so much easier to remember where all the children are and I have a feeling for each child about how much more experience within each region they will need before moving on.'

(An Oxfordshire teacher, 1990)

- The main purpose of assessment is for you to be able to offer the right kinds of experiences to your children. It doesn't need to be onerous.
- Make some assessments about *how* children are approaching their tasks – how involved they are in their learning. Target one or two children for some specially motivating, real-life or 'personal to them' activities. Help them to make choices and to use their own ideas.
- Do the minimum testing. Focusing on 'right and wrong' can damage a child's development as an intelligent learner.

'Getting it wrong stimulates new insights in [...] mathematical problem solving. But this can only be an insightful process if error is not threatening but seen by the learner and the teacher as a source of new discoveries.'

(Marian Whitehead)

The more testing we do, the more children will see errors and mistakes as negative, undesirable parts of learning.

WAYS FORWARD TO DEVELOP COMMUNICATION WITH PARENTS

'Albeit with the best of intentions, parents can exert undesirable pressure on teachers to introduce written recording in mathematics ...'

(Cockcroft, 1982)

'A premature start on formal, written arithmetic is likely to delay progress rather than hasten it.'

(Cockcroft, 1982)

- Encourage children to make their own records of practical work, in their own way, so that parents can see that some mathematics is done.
- Make the mathematics within children's activities explicit so that they can go home and *say* what mathematics they did.
- Let children take activities home to share with a member of their family. This is especially good for any games, puzzles, problems or investigations that have thoroughly engaged the child's interest.
- Create letters, newsletters, booklets, etc. describing the unrecorded mathematics done in the early years at school, or share with parents a copy of your scheme of work for year 1.
- Set up events such as open days, parents' evenings or mathematics assemblies (see chapter 6).
- Invite parents and grandparents to come into school to work alongside young children when they are involved in mathematical games or other activities.
- Get parents involved in setting up a mathematics games library (see page 128).
- Involve parents in decisions and ideas about the records that are shared between home and school. How could they be more useful?

10

TEACHING

'In an external respect, it is easy to perceive when the moment has arrived that one ought to let the child walk alone … the art is to be constantly present and yet not to be present, to let the child be allowed to develop itself, while nevertheless one has constantly a survey clearly before one. The art is to leave the child to itself in the very highest measure and on the greatest possible scale, and to express this apparent abandonment in such a way that, unobserved, one at the same time knows everything …'

(Soren Kierkegaard, 1813–1855)

There is no point at which teachers become perfect. There is only a journey during which we will often try out new ideas, make mistakes, make priorities and try something else. No one can offer exactly the right learning experiences to each child, in all subjects, at every moment in the school day. For the children are all developing, learning and thinking in different ways and at different rates. Perfect teaching, in my view, is much more like learning itself: a process of thinking, decision making, trying things out, reflecting on what works and what doesn't, creating or seeking out new ways to do things, using your imagination, having the self-confidence to enjoy *not* knowing everything and to want to find out more. You can be a perfect teacher, in this sense, whatever your age and experience!

To be continuously developing and challenging ourselves like this puts us on the track of learning professionally. It makes teaching into the pleasure that young children have in their learning. (All the basic principles of learning on page 7 will apply to us as teachers.) In the classroom, this means that you and the children 'resonate' as learners together. It is so important for them to hear us say things like:

'I don't know.'
'Oh, dear! I didn't expect *that* to happen!'
'I really should've given you a lot more time for that, shouldn't I?'
'Can you help me sort out this problem?'

This must go right to the heart of the learning. If a child is struggling, misbehaving, worried, making too many mistakes or uninterested in their work then we must take responsibility for it, reflect on why this might be and do something about it. (It is all too easy to blame the child for being naughty or lazy or of low ability.) Did we offer a task that was too hard? Did they have enough choice? Doesn't it relate to their own experience enough? Of course, all children can have bad days (and all teachers too!) and it is possible that the problem is nothing to do with the task (e.g. illness, problems at home). But generally, the ideal is to provide learning experiences (tasks, activities, etc.) that capture and engage children's curiosity and intellect, making them so engrossed and enthusiastic that they don't even think about misbehaving.

'The problem created so much interest and intense discussion that none of the group left the classroom during playtime.'

(Mulholland, 1992)

'Many five-year-olds show an amazing ability to work and concentrate for long periods of time when they are involved and interested.'

(Wendla Kernig, 1986)

'When pupils are engaged both mentally and physically, behavioural problems seem to diminish.'

(Marilyn Burns, 1990)

This doesn't mean that there are no rules or rigorous discipline. Classroom rules can be agreed with the children (using their ideas for rules, too) so that everyone is able to become involved in their learning without hindrance. Children can be involved, too, in deciding and planning what work to do. (John Ingram (1992) shows that 'seven- and eight-year-olds were able to negotiate in partnership with their teacher a curriculum that was balanced and met the requirements of the National Curriculum in terms of time allocation and attainment targets for English, mathematics and science. They [...] were able to self-organise, plan and resource these activities.' I believe Key Stage 1 children can take part in this too.)

   If we must take full responsibility for children not being engrossed in their work, then there is a danger of teachers feeling even more inadequate than ever before. The important thing is to decide when you can realistically look at your collection of tasks/ activities (as a priority) to find ways of making some of them more 'open' and/or more related to the children's experiences. In the meantime, just accept that some of the activities aren't personally engaging enough and that by making serious plans to develop them in the future, you are a thinking, learning, 'perfect' teacher!

'Conscientiousness often leads teachers into a cycle of self-reproach for the unachieved.'

(Janet Moyles, 1992)

Self-reproach can lead to despondency which will infect the atmosphere of learning in the classroom. Turn yourself around and look at all those problems as challenges for the future, making plans to tackle them and then halving what you expect to achieve in any given time so that it becomes realistic.

Force yourself to write down thirty-five good things about your teaching. (The more despondent you are, the more you need to force yourself to do it.)

How many of your good points relate to the teaching of mathematics?

The closest you are to teaching mathematics with Using and Applying is probably when you are at your best as a teacher: interacting with your children in your favourite subject (i.e. the area of the curriculum you feel most confident about); thoroughly enjoying listening to their ideas; helping them to try things out for themselves; not minding at all that you may not be sure where it will lead; encouraging them to think, reflect, ask questions, explain, reconsider, draft, redraft, explore ...; confident that they are developing their ideas and understanding themselves within a supportive environment (i.e. learning as described in chapter 1). If you can relax enough about mathematics to be more like this, then Using and Applying will come flooding into your teaching. It helps, of course, if the activities themselves are open enough and/or have real purposes or reasons to do them (see pages 110–11 and chapter 7).

As part of their training to be mathematicians, children need to know what is important about mathematics. When they do something particularly mathematical, we need to make it explicit to them (and to the others). Reinforce anything you notice at any time that shows signs of mathematical thinking. For example:

- looking for/finding patterns ... noticing things*;
- deciding something themselves (what to use, how);
- reasoning (if we do this, it might work because ...)*;
- explaining or recording clearly (we know there aren't any more because ...);
- predicting (saying what might/might not happen and why)*;
- reflecting/evaluating/thinking back over how they did something;

- getting 'unstuck' (not minding when something didn't work and trying something else);
- conjecturing (wondering what would happen if ...)*;
- discussing their work intelligently with each other;
- checking something themselves;
- planning/organising themselves.

(*These are especially mathematical.)

'Omair found a pattern in our carpet I'd never seen before. Look ... how could you describe ...? *It's so good to notice patterns yourselves like this. It's being a real mathematician!*'

'Alice began with twos, then she tried threes and fours. Suddenly she thought it would be fun to try ones or zeros! Then she wondered what would happen with hundreds! *It's good to try things out like this in mathematics.*'

'Claire decided for herself to go and get those buttons to help her to find out which squiggly line was longer. *That's a really good thing to do to decide something for yourself like that. She didn't come and ask me what to do.*'

The purpose of public comments like these is not to give praise to the people involved, but instead to help the children to see what real mathematics is all about. It is the mathematical thinking or process of working that is attended to instead of any end results. How children approach their work is so much more important than any outcomes. Children are also experiencing mathematics naturally, within many activities at school (including play). They need us to focus on this mathematics from time to time, in order to relate a particular concept explicitly to their direct experiences (as described in section A).

'Prediction as a learning strategy is easy to encourage. All one has to do is say "Wait! Don't do it yet. Tell me first what you think is going to happen".'

(David Fielker, 1992)

Asking 'open' questions, such as 'What do *you* think?', 'How did you work it out?', 'Is that what you expected? Why?' and 'What could you try next?' help to prompt the children to think for themselves. It's important to take their suggestions and ideas very seriously and to allow them to proceed, even when you know that something won't work. This is one of the hardest things for a teacher to do – resisting the urge to step in when the children are heading for problems. We need to let children make mistakes and learn for themselves. Otherwise, we will slip back into leading questions and closed questions, which take the control for the learning away from the child.

Our questioning needs to challenge the mathematics that we can *see* is correct just as much as the mathematics that includes errors (or simply needs explaining): 'Are you sure?! *How* sure?', 'How did you do this?', 'Have you checked it?'

It also must allow children to have the courage to say what they really think. For example, in asking children to estimate how many apples are in a bag, there may be an amazing range of responses from five to 100 or more. The estimates should all be accepted equally and then the apples can be counted together (and further estimates offered during the counting: 'Does anyone want to change their minds?'). You can observe and assess from this kind of activity, and the children can all learn from the task itself (i.e. the estimating and the counting). They do not actually *need* you to get in the way with your judgements on their efforts. If you start to give praise for the sensible estimates, then the lack of praise can become an issue for those children who realise that they must have 'got it wrong'. They are *all* learning, using every bit of experience at their disposal.

As explained in chapter 1, children who are engaged in true learning, for its own sake, do not need praise (or stars or badges). In fact, too much praise can get in the way of learning, because the children start working to please you instead of for the interest in the task itself, and consequently become less independent learners. (This doesn't mean, of course, that we shouldn't be totally honest with children when our judgements or opinions *are* required.)

As far as possible, children should correct their own (or each other's) mistakes by reflecting back on their work, checking and looking for inconsistencies. Children should build up a whole repertoire of ways to check their work themselves (e.g. using calculators, cubes, estimation and approximation, each other, etc.) and time must be allowed for this. We must not be afraid to have high expectations of young children's ability to think and check for themselves. High expectations of children's learning also allow ambiguity and confusion into their mathematics. We can trust them to ask questions and to sort it out using discussion, experiment and energy. A lot of 'messy', real-life mathematics will bring contradictions and things that don't quite fit the rule:

'Is a carrot a cone? Why? Why not?'

'Is this cog a circle? What about the teeth around the edge? Does it matter?'

'What shape is this slice of bread?'

Different published schemes use different words and ways of presenting the same mathematics. Different teachers use different methods to teach the same aspects of mathematics. Children need this variety and can use it to gain a better understanding of the concepts involved, as long as such variations are noticed and discussed. Real confusion comes from over-simplifying and over-protecting the learner from things that 'don't fit the rule'. The child then tries to apply something to a new context, and it doesn't work out neatly, causing confusion. By putting aspects of mathematics into a wide variety of contexts with real purposes or reasons to explore within each one, children will begin to make the connections that build genuine mathematical understanding.

So far, I have outlined the teachers role as:

- learning and challenging yourself all the time (showing the children that you are learning too, and making priorities and plans for your own development);
- creating an atmosphere for learning based upon responsibility, independence, choice, support, trust, discussion, exploration, thought, imagination and use of children's own ideas;
- encouraging prediction and other mathematical thinking processes by drawing attention to them as they arise;
- resisting the urge to step in when children are heading for problems or mistakes;
- asking 'open' questions to stimulate children's *own* thinking, not closed or leading questions which serve to get the child to follow *our* thinking;
- questioning mathematics that is correct so that children challenge themselves to justify and explain their work;
- not giving too much praise;
- creating activities that are engaging and interesting in their own right (e.g. by allowing choices or relating to the children's own experiences);
- ensuring that the children check their own work wherever possible;
- having high expectations of young children as intelligent learners;
- providing a variety of activities (including 'real-life' ones) for each aspect of mathematics.

It is easy to mock the philosophy of this book and attach labels of 'progressive', 'facilitatory', 'enabling', etc. All these terms have been brought into public disrepute in recent years, in favour of 'formal', 'back to basics', 'traditional', 'didactic', etc.

I make no apology for any of them, but must specify that they are all working *within* a set of rigourously defined Programmes of Study for mathematics. The children's learning is *not* left to chance. Teachers will provide starting points, activities and ideas to engage children's interest and learning within regions of mathematics. They will interact with children, whether as individuals, groups or as a class, to promote children's thinking and understanding by asking open questions and allowing children the freedom to explore. It can't all come from either teacher or child. It is a partnership where both contribute ideas and then negotiate the learning so that curriculum coverage is achieved.

It is enforced by government legislation that all mathematics is now taught through the medium of Using and Applying, which requires children to: make their own decisions; develop a variety of approaches; organise and check their own work; think for themselves; discuss; ask questions; make predictions. These things are totally incompatible with a traditional, didactic teaching style. You cannot tell a child what to do and how to do it if they are supposed to be making their own decisions. You cannot tell them what questions to ask. Using and Applying Mathematics provides a framework or structure for 'child-centred' or 'progressive' teaching. The 'basics' in terms of calculating skills are addressed through Using and Applying Numbers in a totally new way. We now have the best of both worlds, if we can come to terms with allowing initiative, imagination, creativity and confidence into mathematics – exactly those qualities which are not respected, for example, in our traditional, formal, didactic, romantic village school in France.

EPILOGUE

I have always loved making up stories with children that involve them as characters, just disguised enough so that it isn't them. My classroom stories include all sorts of things that have really been happening a few moments before. They then start to describe what's happening at that time, and lead into what might happen next. (When the children are really 'clued in', they make it happen as we progress!). Stories with my children at home are now all based around 'Baby bear' who mirrors their own lives (with just enough differences to claim that it isn't them). Children seem to love these stories so much that I have puzzled for some time over how to publish an equivalent. But of course it is impossible. The trick is in relating everything to themselves, their lives and their surroundings.

I have had a similar problem in designing and writing this book. It can never be directly personal and relevant to you. I have made assumptions about teachers that will not always be true of you. Do send your ideas and suggestions to me for how to improve this book for any future editions! I put myself alongside you and all your children as a learner, first and foremost.

RECOMMENDED READING

CHAPTER 1 AND CHAPTER 10 – LEARNING AND TEACHING

Holt, John *Learning All the Time*, Education Now Publishing Cooperative Limited, Lighthouse Books, 1989

I cannot emphasise strongly enough the importance of John Holt's philosophy of learning. This is his last book, published after his death in 1985, and alongside his other works will probably be the best and most interesting educational reading you will find. Ever.

Holt, John *How Children Fail*, Revised Edition, Penguin Books, (1982)

Holt, John *How Children Learn*, Revised Edition, Penguin Books, (1983)

CHAPTER 2 – UNDERSTANDING MATHEMATICS

Bird, Marion *Mathematics for Young Children – An Active Thinking Approach*, Routledge, 1991

Marion Bird describes six open-ended starting points for number work (case studies) with reception children and analyses the mathematical thinking involved alongside her role as a teacher. An excellent book for gaining an insight into 'managing' open-ended mathematics with very young children so that the children themselves are in control of their explorations.

Burton, Leone *Children Learning Mathematics: Patterns and Relationships*, Simon & Schuster, 1994

Excellent on how primary children can be in control of their learning of mathematics and our changing perception of mathematics as teachers. More academic than practical.

PrIME *Calculators, Children and Mathematics. The Calculator-Aware Number Curriculum*, NCC, Simon & Schuster, 1991

A clear account of the CAN Curriculum from 1986 to 1989 with teachers' comments and children's work. It describes and represents the way number work should be taught for the future, especially in Key Stage 1. Essential reading.

Haylock and Cockburn *Understanding Early Years Mathematics*, Paul Chapman, 1989

A book that enables Key Stage 1 teachers to gain a better understanding of mathematics.

Skemp, Richard R. *Mathematics in the Primary School*, Routledge, 1989

Excellent on ideas/analogies about what 'real' mathematics is and how best to learn it.

CHAPTER 3, CHAPTER 4 AND CHAPTER 5 – THE HIDDEN MATHEMATICS CURRICULUM

The Mathematical Association *Maths Talk*, Stanley Thornes Ltd. Second Edition (National Curriculum) 1992

This book is highly readable and helpful in seeing the links between speaking and listening and mathematics. It is excellent in exploring mathematical discussion, with plenty of practical ideas and ways forward.

Straker, Anita *Talking Points in Mathematics* Cambridge University Press, 1993

An excellent book full of ideas to support five or more minutes of talking about mathematics. The introductory section of the book is extremely useful for planning and organising discussion.

Walsh, Angela (ed.) *Help Your Child with Mathematics*, BBC, 1988.

The book of the BBC series, aimed at parents of four- to eleven-year-olds, but good for teachers too. Offers everyday activities and opportunities for mathematics and a useful list of books with mathematical themes.

CHAPTERS 6, CHAPTER 7 AND CHAPTER 8 – THE MATHEMATICS CURRICULUM TIME

Richards, Roy and Jones, Lesley *An Early Start to Mathematics*, Simon and Schuster, 1990

Many good ideas under National Curriculum headings. Extremely accessible, colourful and easy to use.

BEAM *Starting from...*, Series Resource Books for Teachers, BEAM, Barnsbury Complex, Offord Road, London N1 1QH, tel. 0171–457 5533.

A whole series of 'ideas books' for intriguing and enjoyable Using and Applying mathematics activities. Many books are relevant (or based on) Key Stage 1.

Atkinson, Sue (ed.) *Mathematics with Reason*, Hodder and Stoughton, 1992

A series of contributions about introducing symbols, children's own methods, problem solving and exploring mathematics. Very accessible and easy to read.

Ebbutt, Sheila and Straker, Anita *Children and Mathematics Part 1*, ILEA, 1988.

Excellent on working with a calculator, computer, problem solving, etc. Very clear and helpful.

SELECTED BIBLIOGRAPHY

Anno, M. (1975) *Anno's Counting Book*, Macmillan, 1979

ATM. (1991) *Exploring Mathematics with younger children*

Baratta-Lorton, M. (1976) *Mathematics Their Way*, Addison-Wesley

Brown, R. (1977) 'Introduction' in C. Snow and C. Ferguson (eds) *Talking to Children: From Input to Acquisition*, Cambridge University Press

Burningham, J. (1978) *Would You Rather?* Jonathan Cape

Burns, M. (1987 USA, 1990 UK) *A collection of maths lessons for the Primary Classroom*, Learning Development Aids (LDA)

Burton, L. (1992) 'Do young children think mathematically?' *Early Child Development and Care*, **82**, pp. 57–63

Carles, E. (1991) *A Wild Herb Soup: The Life of a French Countrywoman*, Gollancz

Child Education (June 1994 to March 1995), Scholastic

Clarke, S. (January/ February 1994) 'Progress and Purpose' in *Strategies* **4**, 3

Clemson, D. and Clemson, W. (1994) *Mathematics in the Early Years*, Routledge

Cockcroft, W. *et al.* (1982) *Mathematics Counts*, HMSO

Cornelius, G. and Casler, J. (1991) 'Enhancing creativity in young children: Strategies for teachers' in *Early Child Development and Care*, **72**, pp. 99–106

Denvir, B and Brown, M. (1986) 'Understanding of mathematical concepts in low-attaining 7–9 year olds.' *Educational Studies in Mathematics Education*, **17**, pp. 143–64

Department for Education (January 1995) *Key Stages 1 and 2 of the National Curriculum*, HMSO

Donaldson, M. (1978) *Children's Minds*, Fontana Press

Doughty, V. (February 1995) 'Home Sweet Home', *Child Education*, **72**, 2, pp. 16, 17

Duffin, J. (February 1992) 'No fear of figures', *Strategies*, **2**, 2

Duffin J. (1993) *Calculators in the Classroom*, Homerton College and Mathematical Association, Hilary Shuard Memorial Funds

Early Years Curriculum Group (1991) *Early Childhood Education*

Early Years Curriculum Group (1993) *Early Education in Jeopardy. An action paper for early years practitioners*, Action Paper Number 1

Early Years Curriculum Group (1992) 'First Things First: educating young children: a guide for parents and governors.'

Fielker, D. (May/June 1994) 'Ambiguities and decisions', *Strategies*, **4**, 5, p.23

Frobisher, L. J. (1992) 'Towards a unified approach to teaching and learning mathematics.' *Early Child Development and Care*, **82**, pp. 5–26

HMI (1989) 'The Education of Children Under Five', *Aspects of Primary Education*, DES

Hughes, M. (1986) *Children and Number. Difficulties in Learning Maths*, Blackwell

ILEA (1988) *The Early Years – A Curriculum for Young Children*

ILEA (1988) *Mathematics in ILEA Primary Schools: Children and Mathematics, A Handbook for Teachers*

Kanji *et al.* (1990) *The Early Years: a curriculum for young children*

Keslake, D. (October 1993) 'Context – What context?' *Strategies,* **4**, 1

Liebeck, P (1984) *How Children Learn Mathematics,* Pelican

Liebschner, J. (Autumn 1993) 'The Curriculum of Friedrich Froebel. Edited Highlights from Froebel's Writings,' *Early Years,* **14**, 1

MacNamara, A. (1992) 'How Many Are There?' *Early Years,* **13**, 1

Mosley, F. (1989) *Help Your Child Learn Number Skills.* Usborne Parents' Guides

Moyles, J. (1992) *Organising for Learning in the Primary Classroom,* Open University Press

Mulholland, V. (1992) 'Mathematics across the curriculum', *Early Child Development and Care,* **82**, pp. 37–47

NCC 'Using and Applying' Book A

NCC 'Using and Applying' Book B, Supplementary Reading 5: Issues in Progression

NCC (1989) *Mathematics Non-Statutory Guidance,* DES HMSO

OFSTED (1993) *The teaching and learning of number in primary schools,* HMSO

OFSTED (1993) *First Class – The Standards and Quality of Education in Reception Classes,* HMSO

OFSTED (1991–1992) *Mathematics Key Stages 1, 2 and 3,* Third Year

Oxfordshire County Council (1990) Mathematics Advisory Support Team, 'Activities Towards' Series

Oxfordshire County Council, Mathematics Advisory Support Team (1991) *Teacher Assessment Activities for Mathematics at Key Stages 1 and 2*

Palmer and Pettit (1993) *Topic work in the early years* (Organising the Curriculum for 4–8 year olds), Routledge

Pascoe, E. (October 1994) 'It's never too late to get a life!' SHE, p. 116

SCAA (School Curriculum and Assessment Authority) (1991–93) *Evaluation of the Implementation of National Curriculum Mathematics at Key Stage 1, 2 and 3,* Summary Report

Shuard, H. (July 1991) 'We can work it out', *Strategies* **1**, 5

Skemp, R. (1989) 'Structured Activities for Primary Mathematics: How to Enjoy Real Mathematics' Volume 1: For the early years

Sugarman, I. (July 1994) 'Children calculating,' *Strategies* **4**, 6 pp. 28–30

Threlfall, J. (June 1992) 'No Sums Please, We're Infants.' *Education 3–13,* **20**, 2, pp. 15–17

Tizard, B and Hughes, M. (1984) *Young Children Learning,* Fontana Press

Walland, H. (November/December 1993) 'The art of the possible', In *Strategies,* **4**, 2

Walsh, A. (1992) 'The calculator as a catalyst for change', *Early Child Development and Care,* **82**, pp. 49–56

Whitebread, D. (January 1995) *et al.* 'Infant Newshounds', *Child Education,* **72**, 1, pp. 29–36

Whitehead, M. (1992) 'Assessment at Key Stage 1: Core Subjects and the Developmental Curriculum', Chapter 5 of *Assessment in Early Childhood Education* by Blenkin, G. and Kelly A, Paul Chapman Publishing